XI

D1273267

DATE DUE

CANNON
FODDER

CANNON FODDER

An
Infantryman's Life
on the Western Front
1914–18

A. STUART DOLDEN

BLANDFORD PRESS
Poole   Dorset

First published in the U.K. 1980

Copyright © 1980 Blandford Press Ltd.,
Link House, West Street,
Poole, Dorset, BH15 1LL

British Library Cataloguing in Publication Data

Dolden, Stuart
  Cannon fodder.
  1. European War, 1914-1918 – Campaigns –
  Western   2. European War, 1914-1918 –
  Personal narratives, British   3. Great
  Britain. Army. London Scottish Regiment
  I. Title
  940.4'144'0924   D547.L6

ISBN 0 7137 1108 6

Typeset in 11/12½ pt V.I.P.
Garamond by Tonbridge Printers
Printed and Bound in Great Britain by
Biddles of Guildford

Contents

Preface		7
Author's Note		8

1914 – 15

1	Early days–Embarkation–Rouen	10
2	No. 4. Entrenching Battalion	15
3	The Trenches at Vermelles	19
4	Divisional Rest at Lespesse	24
5	The Battle of Loos	27
6	The Battle of Hulloch	37
7	Rest at Lillers	48
8	No. 26 General Hospital	52

1916

9	Return to Battalion–Leaving 1st Division	58
10	The 56th Division	60
11	Villers sur Simon	63
12	St. Amand–Halloy–Souastre–Hébuterne	68
13	Opening of Battle of The Somme	71
14	The Somme	81
15	The Armentières Sector	93

1917

16	The Armentières Sector (continued)	104
17	Arras	112
18	Simoncourt–Archicourt–Moule–Liencourt	123
19	Ypres–Le Transloy–Lagnicourt	126
20	Ecurie–Roclincourt–Vimy Ridge–Maroeuil	133

1918

21	The Great German Offensive	138
22	The Arras Caves–Blangy–Feuchy	149
23	Château de la Haie —Tilloy —Boiry —Boyelles	157
24	Cambrai	164
25	The Final German Retreat	170

Index	183

*This book is dedicated to
the 'Old Comrades' past and present
with whom I served in World War I.*

Preface

War is a ghastly business, and none more so than World War I. The lot of the Infantrymen was a far from envious one, and the way in which they were handled was, quite understandably, the reason that they have been referred to as 'CANNON FODDER'. Despite the gruesomeness of war in general, life also had its lighter side. This is the story of one who is proud to have served in the ranks with the 1st Battalion London Scottish Regiment, in France and Belgium. This book is based on a day to day diary that I kept during the War, and all the incidents referred to therein were recorded at the time or very soon after the event, and nothing has been left to the imagination.

The keeping of a diary by a private soldier was generally regarded to be against King's Regulations. Consequently, I was only able to use small notebooks and very often just sheets of paper that I could carry in the breast pocket of my tunic. I still have these notebooks in my possession together with the sheets of paper and, as a matter of interest to readers, included in the book is a reproduction of one of my experiences on 13 October 1915, during the attack on the Hollenzollern Redoubt at Hulloch.

A. Stuart Dolden, 1980

Author's Note

The expression 'P.O.B. . . . 'D' Company mentioned in this book needs some explanation. At one time we had a CQMS who was rather partial to the rum ration. Consequently, when it came to the distribution of rations, or the allocation of billets, the CQMSs of the other Companies were able to pull a fast one over him, and the result was that we always seemed to get the worst billets. It may have been coincidence, but if any distasteful work had to be done 'D' Company seemed to 'click'. When this had been going on for some time, our CSM was heard to exclaim Poor Old B . . . 'D'. That phrase stuck and ever since, and indeed long after, the Company has always been known as POBD and members of the Company during the War feel very proud of this and look upon the words almost as a decoration, for they feel that they have earned it the hard way.

E.S.D.

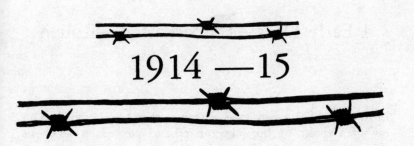

1914 —15

1 Early Days—Embarkation—Rouen

In the year 1909, when I was sixteen years of age, I embarked on my life's career by becoming an articled clerk in a solicitor's office. Approximately four and a half years later, in June 1914, I passed my Law Final examination. As I had to complete five years of my articles, I was not able to obtain my certificate to practice until November 1914, when I was appointed an Assistant Solicitor in the Legal Department at Liverpool Street Station of the old Great Eastern Railway.

A few days later I announced at breakfast that I was going to join the Army. I sensed from my parents' silence that they were not too keen on the idea. However, they did not say anything to deter me. I was of a slight and not robust build, and one of my brothers' friends expressed the opinion that 'I would not stay the course', so with this depressing thought I set off to 59 Buckingham Gate, in south-west London, with the object of joining the London Scottish Regiment. The only time that I had been in their drill hall previously was when I attended the Enquiry into the Titanic disaster and had heard Chief Officer Lightoller give his evidence.

I took my place in the queue with a number of others wishing to volunteer, and eventually found myself in front of the Medical Officer. When I was turned down on the grounds that my chest measurement was two inches under requirement, I felt absolutely shattered, and decided there and then that something had to be done about it. Accordingly I went to a Physical Culture Centre in Dover Street, London, which was run by a Dane called Muller. In consultation he informed me that he would accept me for his course, and then I put my foot in it by asking him how much it would cost! Apparently the Maestro was far above considerations of money and referred me to his secretary, a far more down to earth gentleman. He informed me that the course consisted of ten half-hourly sessions, the fee for which was twenty guineas (£21.00). This was a considerable sum in those days. He also told me that many famous people had taken the course, including the then Archbishop of Canterbury and General French. I told him that I was not concerned with these gentlemen since it was my father who would have to foot the bill, and I knew he would not pay twenty guineas! After a lot of talk about doing it from a patriotic motive he asked if my father would pay eight guineas, so I said I doubted it, but I would see what he said.

Now I was in a quandary because I had to get my father's consent. I went to his office and told a tale that I must be in a bad way, and something would have to be done about it. I did not say in so many words, but I gave the impression that I was bordering on consumption. My father listened and remained silent for some time, and then said I should give the secretary a ring and ask if he would be prepared to accept six guineas. Like a shot I got on to the telephone to the secretary and explained the position, and to my great relief he agreed and told me to come in the morning. Next day I arrived there only to find that the course was spread over three months. I said straight away that that was no good, and that I must do it in ten days. After a great deal of eye raising it was agreed. I had an individual instructor and no apparatus was used, for the treatment consisted merely of deep breathing, in conjunction with the appropriate manual exercises. The tenth day arrived, and to my great relief my chest had attained the required two inches in expansion.

Back I went to 59 Buckingham Gate the next day and, not disclosing I had been before, I again confronted the Medical Officer. This time I sailed through with flying colours, and after swearing the Oath of Allegiance, I found myself a soldier on one shilling (5p) a day pay. I also had to pay one pound for the privilege of joining the London Scottish Regiment. At the time I thought this rather odd, but looking back over the years I realise that in view of the bond of comradeship created during the War, and which has continued ever since, that it was indeed a privilege to have belonged to such a Regiment.

I was now about to commence my training, and at first travelled daily from my home to headquarters. The training facilities were somewhat restricted in London, and we seemed to spend most of our time marching to Richmond Park, Hampstead Heath, or round and round Regent's—Park there closely watched

11

by the monkeys from London Zoo, who no doubt were wondering just what it was all about!

On 9 March 1915, after being issued with uniforms and kitted out, I went with a draft of three hundred other recruits to Dorking in Surrey to join the 2nd Battalion. Some time later we left for Watford from where, after a stay of some time, we started on a march for Saffron Walden in Essex via North Mimms, Hatfield, where we spent the night in the stables of Hatfield House and then continued on to Hertford, Much Hadham, Bishop's Stortford, until finally on 20 May we arrived at Saffron Walden.

Every soldier was supplied with an identity disc to be worn round his neck, on which was embossed his name, number, regiment and religion. A member of my Company, one Eastwood, when asked for his religion replied 'What are you short of?' He finally settled for Roman Catholic in the belief that as we were a Scottish regiment he would not have to attend church parades. But alas! The following Sunday he was mustered and marched off with other Roman Catholics to a service about five miles away. On Monday he changed his religion; I have never seen such a dramatic conversion, and all without the aid of prayer!

Our guard room was in an empty shop in the town. I was on guard outside in the early hours of one morning, when I heard someone approaching with a great deal of noise, and round the corner appeared a London Scot who hailed from South Africa, and who was obviously the worse for drink. He was cracking a sjambok, a whip used in the old days by the Boers to control their teams of eight oxen harnessed to a wagon. It was a long whip with a vicious thong at the tip. He spotted me and thought, no doubt, he would scare the daylights out of me . . . and he succeeded. I knew, however, that it would be fatal to show it, so I kept rigidly still. He continued cracking the whip in ever narrowing circles, till finally the thong was just missing my nose by an inch, and at this stage he possibly thought that his efforts to scare me had failed, so turned round and sailed off into the night still shouting and cracking his murderous whip!

A large draft was formed, in which I was included, destined for the 1st Battalion in France. We were entitled to four days embarkation leave, but at the last moment this was cancelled. We left Saffron Walden by train and after a circuitous route arrived at Southampton where we were encamped on a common. We spent four days there waiting for transport, and at last on 5 July 1915 the call came. In glorious sunshine we marched from our camp to the docks in a triumphal procession, and as we passed the dock gates they slammed to with a clang, as if to say 'There is no turning back'. For us the great adventure had begun.

We waited on the quay for two hours, and then embarked on board the transport steamer *Sipkah*, an old cattle boat, and at 5.20pm we set sail with aeroplanes passing over and around us.

We passed through a boom, and later picked up a naval escort of two torpedo boat destroyers which went round us in circles during the Channel crossing. Darkness came, along with strict instructions that there was to be no smoking or showing of lights. Lifebelts were issued out to us and I then found a place in the hold to sleep. Two things rather marred my comfort, however; one was the hardness of the boards, and the other the overpowering aroma in the air. Judging by the strength thereof, the previous occupants must have been horses and in fact there was ample evidence on the floor to confirm my suspicions.

Early next morning I went on deck just in time to see our escort return to England, and a French destroyer take over. We steamed into Le Havre, and after about ten hours set off again up the river Seine to Rouen. As by then it was well after dark, we slept the night on board. We were up again at 5am next morning, and each of us received tea and was issued with one hundred and twenty rounds of ammunition. We disembarked two and a half hours later, and marched to a camp near the race course about four miles outside the town. There, tents were allotted to us, and after inspection by the Officer commanding the camp and the Medical Officer, we were dismissed for the day.

The camp held about eighty thousand men, and included an Indian section and hospitals. We spent a month there during which the usual training was carried out, on the Cavalry parade ground about a mile from the camp. Trenches and dugouts had been made with barbed wire entanglements in front, and there we carried out those weird and wonderful manoeuvres pertaining to Army warfare.

There were lectures from time to time on various subjects, and the one that stamped itself most vividly on my mind was one on lice, ably given by a sergeant who had been in the trenches on the Western Front and was therefore fully qualified to speak on the subject. He suggested several remedies to keep free from vermin, but apparently the only effective means was to burn everything; this did not seem to me to be a very practical suggestion.

The usual fatigues had to be performed, and on two occasions I was detailed with Walker under Corporal Faulkner to go to the Refreshment Room at the Rive Gauche railway station in Rouen. This room was set apart entirely as a canteen for troops going up the line, and I spent my time collecting dirty cups, washing up, cleaning out bottles and carrying awkward parcels. Our duties over, we returned to camp in an ambulance.

Efforts had been made to beautify the camp, and in front of some of the Officer's quarters little gardens had been planted with flowers and vegetables, and in some cases regimental crests and badges had been worked with various pieces of coloured glass to give quite an artistic touch.

The water supply was somewhat erratic, a serious matter to us in those early days, because it meant that if one was absent at the proper time it would be hours before you could get a wash. The water system seemed to work only when the spirit moved it, but, as our experience ripened, we learned just when to be on the spot 'when the waters moved'.

'All work and no play makes Jack a dull boy' it is said, and we therefore had time off for recreation. A great deal of our spare moments were spent in the YMCA hut where we were able to obtain refreshments, play billiards and from time to time listen to concerts arranged by the various regiments and others.

2 No. 4 Entrenching Battalion

On 18 July 1915 a Battalion was formed from the various drafts in the camp, including the contingent from the London Scottish, to form what was known as Number Four Entrenching Battalion, or as we preferred to call it 'The Navvies' Battalion'. This formation was to be used for digging trenches near the line. About forty of the Scottish were drafted to this Battalion and we were very sore at being put into this unit, as we wanted to go up the line to our Regiment. We held a meeting and, as a result, sent a letter to the Officer commanding, asking him to consider our case. At the conclusion of the parade next day we were informed that we were only to be drafted to the Entrenching Battalion until such time as our own Regiment required reinforcements, and the fact of being in the Entrenching Battalion would not delay our getting to our own Regiment. This calmed our fears somewhat, and we felt more assured about everything.

On 5 August there were signs of our removal from Rouen. The deficiences in our kit were made up, bully beef and biscuits were served out, and at 6.15pm we moved off in full marching order to the railway station at Rouen. On arrival we boarded the longest train that I have ever seen, longer than three English trains put together. We left just after 9pm, at a speed that could only be described as dead slow. I endeavoured to get some sleep, but it seemed as though everyone was on top of me, for as there were six of us with full marching kit, packs included, space was somewhat limited.

On awakening next morning at about 4am we found ourselves at Abbeville, but, instead of stopping, the train continued its journey until eventually about 10.15am we arrived at Doullens where we detrained, and marched off in heavy rain to a small camp about five miles from the town. All the tents had been daubed with paint to form camouflage against enemy aircraft. We stayed there for a time and then after packs had been handed in to be carried by the transport, set off again on a ten mile march, until we arrived at the small village of Varennes, where we were billeted in an antiquated barn. I felt absolutely done up, so using my waterproof sheet as a blanket soon turned in for a rest.

The next day we had to ourselves, and so whiled away the time in taking stock of our surroundings, and in talking to French soldiers. After a wash at the farm pump we drew rations of army biscuits, one tin of butter for eight men, and one tin of jam for five men.

On 8 August our serious work began, and our first duty as behoved an entrenching battalion was to draw picks and shovels, for a navvy is not much use without his shovel. We remained at this spot for about eighteen days and each day, Sundays included, dug trenches at a place about a mile and a half from the village. In addition to this were the usual irritating inspections.

The water in the village was bad, and we were forbidden to drink it, so the battalion watercart used to make four journeys daily and returned with water from a good supply for the needs of the battalion.

Our billet had been christened 'The Bug Pit' by previous occupants, and there was a notice to that effect on the door.

One day when I took off my tunic I noticed with a sense of horror that the inevitable had happened—'I was lousy'. I felt like hiding my head in shame, but on looking round furtively, I noticed that all the others were going down the seams of their tunics with lighted cigarettes. After that I felt a bit better and did the same to my seams. I wrote home for a tin of Keatings (at that time a well-known insecticide), but this was of no use; in fact the devils seemed to thrive on it. From the amount of blood that vermin sucked from my body throughout the war, I wondered that I did not become anaemic.

Daily life passed very quietly, and except for the arrival one day of a travelling band in an omnibus to give us a programme of light music, nothing very momentous happened.

On 18 August 'the even tenor of our way' was interrupted by signs of another move. Steel helmets were issued out to us, and also 'Iron Rations' or emergency rations consisting of bully beef, and a tin of groceries and biscuits. The instructions were that the iron rations were not to be eaten unless one had been without food for twenty four hours. Even then, these could only be eaten with the permission given by an Officer.

After a sleepless cold night, we paraded at 4.45am the next morning and a draft, consisting of forty from the London Scottish and thirty from the Highland Light Infantry, marched to Acheux station and there entrained. We travelled on a narrow gauge railway to Gezaincourt Halte where we alighted and marched to a goods yard adjoining the broad gauge track. We again entrained and travelled to Longpré which we reached about two hours later.

After some considerable time we joined another train, and journeyed to Abbeville where we bade farewell to our Highland Light Infantry friends. The train was just on the move again, when someone rushed up and said that the Scottish were to detrain also. Wild pandemonium followed as we threw our packs out of the carriage and, following ourselves, finished our dressing on the ballast. We regaled ourselves at the Expeditionary Force canteen while waiting for our next train and, when this arrived, found that our luck had changed for we had cattle trucks to travel in. Twenty of us were put into each truck, and the noise was so great that we could hardly hear each other speak. Late at night we were shunted into a siding at Lillers. We made ourselves as comfortable as possible, and early next morning took another train and later disembarked at Foucquereuil, our destination, and here we had to wait until called for.

A scout from the 1st Battalion arrived to guide us, and after a very tiring march we arrived at the village of Vermelles, where the 1st Battalion was stationed.

At this time the Regiment was in the 1st Guards Brigade of the 1st Division and consisted of the 1st Coldstream Guards, 1st Scots Guards, 1st Black Watch, 1st Cameron Highlanders and 1st London Scottish.

Vermelles was in an appalling state, for the whole village had been demolished by shellfire, and there was hardly a house left standing. We halted outside the Regimental HQ, some shattered houses, and while waiting to be allocated to Companies, visited a canteen in the cellar of one of the houses that had been destroyed by shell fire. In the yard Royal Artillery guns were blazing away, and on the crossroads outside there was a notice warning that enemy shells often fell there.

At 4pm we heard that we were to go into the trenches and so

sallied forth to join the Battalion. Just as we did so a German shell burst over the village, and after an hour's walk through a communication trench we reached our destination.

3 The Trenches at Vermelles

Four of us were drafted into 'D' Company and were then taken along to the reserve trench to join Number 13 Platoon. We had had our baptism of fire on the way up as shells were bursting around us.

When we arrived at our position the Platoon fellows gave us a hearty welcome and, as we had no rations, and would not have any until the next day, they willingly gave us tea and shared their eatables with us. Thus began my lifelong association with 'D' Company which continued during and after the War. We were next shown to dugouts; I shared with Fraser and when night fell we prepared to turn in. A candle stuck in a little niche in the side of the dugout served as a light, but very little shelter was afforded as it was merely a hole scooped out in the side of the trench, and we lay in it with out legs sticking out into the trench. At 9pm I went on trench guard for an hour, to guard the communication trench that ran to the front line. In the event of an alarm my duty was to pull down sandbags, and so block the trench. A box of bombs was placed in readiness to hold up any of the enemy that might chance to come along. I had not the faintest idea how to work a bomb, as I had never thrown one of them in my life. I loaded my rifle, however, and prepared to keep watch. The Germans were sending up star shells, and as these burst and fluttered to the ground with a sickly pale light they gave the impression 'of a soul passing over'.

This, together with the fact that I had a box of bombs, the mechanism of which I was entirely ignorant, helped to produce a very uncanny and eerie sort of feeling and it was with much relief, therefore, that I eventually came off guard duty and was able to turn into the little dugout 'Curly Crescent', this being the name of the reserve trench.

We had to sleep fully dressed, of course, and with ammunition and equipment on, this was very uncomfortable for the pressure of ammunition on one's chest restricted breathing; furthermore, when a little warmth was obtained the vermin used to get busy, and for some unexplained reason they always seemed to get lively in that portion of one's back, that lay underneath the belt and was the most inaccessible spot. The only way to obtain relief was to get out of the dugout, put a rifle barrel between the belt and back, and rub up and down like a donkey at a gate post. This stopped them for a bit, but as soon as one got back into the dugout, and was getting reasonably warm so would the little brutes get going again.

Breakfast next morning consisted of tea made in the trench on little fires that we lit with odds and ends such as match ends, paper and pieces of wood. There was also bacon, bread and jam which had been sent up with the rations.

Four of us had to report at Battalion HQ, and were then detailed to dig a dugout, and when this was finished we returned to the Company. The journey back took us thirty five minutes as the communication trench was very long and, in fact, I thought we were never going to get to the end of it.

In the evening we went for water, and for this we collected up the fellows' water bottles and also petrol cans which we filled from the water cart at Battalion HQ.

At 10pm the whole Company moved to another position in the trenches somewhere in the neighbourhood of Noyelles, about half a mile to the left of our present position. Another dugout was allotted to us and eleven of us had to sleep in this. The new trench was called 'Pip Street'. There was very little to do next day except to parade for rifle inspection. Two of us had to collect all the empty water tins and return them to HQ, and while we were doing this the Germans began to shell. The shells burst very close, and I got a piece of shrapnel in the back from a 'Whizz Bang'; luckily it only grazed my coat, but it was close enough for a beginning.

In the evening we were relieved by 'C' Company, and so wended our way to the communication trench and, under cover of a hedge, found our way into Vermelles, where we were billeted in what appeared to be the scullery of a house which had been knocked about by gunfire. The roof was good in parts and for these times was quite comfortable. Stew and tea were served out to us on arrival, and we then settled down to spend the evening in a singsong. We had to sleep in our clothes, but as we were not actually in the trenches, we were allowed to remove our ammunition and equipment. We were also given special permission to take off our boots and, as this was the first time for four days, we were mighty glad of the relief.

I was washing at the pump in the yard next morning when German shells came hurtling over; fortunately, however, no-one was hit. We cleaned up the billet, and then adjourned to the underground canteen, and were able later to get a hot bath, a luxury indeed. This was the first hot bath I had been able to have for two months. The bathroom was a room in one of the shelled houses, and four iron baths stood in a row, but the water was only about two inches deep.

In the evening we drew picks and shovels, and prepared to go out to a position in advance of our front line, to dig a trench in 'No Man's Land' near to the German front line. At the last moment, however, we were taken off this job and were put on a carrying fatigue in the charge of our Platoon Commander. We accordingly left the village carrying 'cheveux de frises'. These were barbed wire entanglements made of wood and wire, and were similar to knife rests. Each one was about eight feet long and was carried by two men. As we had rifles and equipment and our way lay over ground honeycombed with shell holes, the carrying proved a ticklish business, and as we were subject every now and then to snipers' bullets, it was not a job with which I was particularly enamoured.

There was also a digging party out in the front and the Germans evidently got wind of it because they began to open up machine gun and rifle fire. Star shells went up and very soon bullets were whizzing about us.

The German snipers were very active, and killed two and wounded five of the Scots Fusiliers. The Camerons had fifteen casualties and the Black Watch several wounded.

On the way up the Hulloch road we had to pass a wayside shrine; this was a favourite spot for snipers and, in fact, they had fixed rifles sighted on the spot so that when darkness fell they had only to touch off the trigger. As we approached a bullet passed over but, thank heavens, we had moved past the shrine before the second one arrived.

Our carrying job took about two hours and we returned to our billets with, fortunately, no casualties in our particular party.

Theoretically, we were supposed to be the Company in reserve, but the next day I was detailed to carry stew to the fellows in the trenches. The Corporal in charge of us lost his way and we trudged laboriously through the trenches for an hour and a half. On our return we cleaned up the billets for moving and, while clearing up outside, three shells burst over us and we had to run like mad for cover. We found out afterwards that an incinerator had been left burning and this had apparently drawn the enemy's fire.

About 7.15pm our Platoon left Vermelles for a rest. We marched to Verquin, and were billeted there in the outbuildings of a colliery. The greatest luxury of all was the electric light; true, it was not brilliant, but it was a step in the right direction. As the Battalion was on two hours alert, in the event of an alarm, we were allowed to undress and this was the first time I had done so for five days. Sleep did not come very easily for the floor of the billet was of stone and, apart from being very hard, sent a chill through one. Moreover at intervals during the night there was a stream of French miners filing passed. The 'Davy' safety lamps were kept in the building in which we were sleeping, and as the old shift came off duty they came in to give up their lamps. The new shift then came along to get lamps before going down the mine. They all had heavy hobnailed boots on and, in addition, they would persist in shouting and talking at the top of their voices. This would not have been so bad, however, had it not been for their objectionable habit of spitting. I do not know whether digging for coal creates more saliva than other occupations, but there did seem to be an unnecessary amount of spitting that night. Fortunately I was not in the line of fire, but others in the Platoon were not so lucky. On getting up next morning we found ourselves covered with a film of coal dust.

During the day I looked round to see if I could find another place to sleep in as I did not relish the experience of the previous night. There were some carts in the yard belonging to the Royal Engineers, and so a few of us took possession of them and, after having covered the top with our waterproof sheets and placed some straw from a stack on the floor, moved our equipment there. It rained heavily during the night, and water dripped through the sheet, but after stopping this things were not so bad. Our clothing got somewhat wet, however, so next day we went along to the engine room of the colliery, and left our things there to dry.

We spent just on a week at Verquin officially resting, but this of course must not be taken too literally, as the time was taken up with the usual drilling, marching and inspections.

I was made a bomber and went on a bombing instruction course at Vaudrecourt, and there in a system of trenches threw dummy bombs.

There was a slag heap in the village from the top of which was a good view of the surrounding country. The German line was clearly visible, as also were the villages of La Basseé, Béthune and Vermelles, but we were sufficiently far enough behind the line to be out of range of shellfire. A German plane came over, but was beaten back by our anti–aircraft guns.

One afternoon a sudden humane reaction very nearly landed me into trouble. We had a Platoon pet, a little terrier that we had picked up in the trenches. In the yard I happened to spot a Frenchman with a little dog which I thought was our Jock; he was dowsing the animal with a hose fitted to a pipe and, as the rush of water was very strong, the pup looked far from happy. This act struck me as being impudent, apart from the unnecessary rough handling, so I dashed over to the pump and, grasping the hose out of the man's hand, turned it full on him and drenched him from head to foot. It was not until then that I realised that the dog belonged to the Frenchman and was not our Jock at all. I must have looked more fearsome than I felt, for the Frenchman took it very calmly and slunk off without a word of protest.

4 Divisional Rest at Lespesse

On 31 August 1915, we left Verquin on a fifteen mile march to Lespesse, a village about four and a half miles south west of Lillers. We were destined to stop there till 21 September going through intensive training for the approaching autumn offensive. The Battalion was billeted in barns and the particular one in which I was put with Number 13 Platoon was filled with straw about half way up to the roof. The march had been a very trying one on account of our heavy packs so that when the opportunity came I, for one, was not loathe to hit the hay.

There was a big opening in a partition through which we could see the cows tied up in their stalls under the same roofs as ourselves. Dreary sounds of lowing occasionally wafted through, and the aroma became somewhat strong at times as the cattle moved about; however, the animals finally settled down and all was peaceful.

The training we went through during the next few weeks was of a fairly gruelling nature, and helped to harden us for the privations ahead. The Battalion went for marches and engaged in practice attacks. Particular attention was directed to a movement known to us as 'belly flopping'—the act of getting down quickly on the ground in a prone position.

We certainly learned to 'flop' in record time, and some of us were to reap the benefit of this training later on. There was a rifle range, and at times we practiced bomb throwing with dummies. There was also a demonstration of the smoke bomb.

One day we had orders to sort through our ammunition, and to pick out those pieces marked 'B'. This appeared to be American–made ammunition that was faulty.

I was standing alone on guard in the early hours one morning, when I heard the sounds of footsteps approaching along the road. Soon I spied a non–commissioned officer in a condition that suggested he had been celebrating. In these circumstances, therefore, I thought it polite not to be seen by him and so quickly moved to the other end of my beat. He hesitated and then seeing the door of the yard attached to our billet open, went in. I then heard sundry muffled curses and, judging by the direction from which the sound emanated, formed the impression that he had fallen into the 'midden'—a spot where all the manure of the farm is stacked! My suspicions were confirmed when he later emerged from the doorway, for his kilt and tunic were in a terrible state. He went off, presumably to his own quarters, carrying part of the midden on him. I thought that the incident was closed, but there was to be a sequel, for next morning there was a voice at the guard room asking for the guard who was on duty the previous night. I went out and found the reveller of the night before, now all clean and spruce. He asked me if I had seen him in the early hours. He obviously had not the slightest notion of what had happened and, not wishing to become involved, I denied all knowledge, whereupon he left. I found out later that the reason for his call was that he had lost his false teeth somewhere the previous evening, and was trying to trace their whereabouts.

On 3 September the whole Battalion was issued with Balmoral headgear and from that date we ceased to wear Glengarries. During the time we were at Lespesse the Battalion was swept by a craze for Rugby football. This is how it came about. One morning an Army Service Corps fellow arrived on a motorcycle; he dismounted and strolled into the billet where he asked Corporal Jones if the Battalion would raise a team to play the Divisional Supply Column at rugger. Jones agreed, a date was fixed and the fellow promised to arrange for motor lorries to take us into Lillers where the match was to be played. He impressed upon us that they were quite a medium team, and we fell for it. Corporal Jones then looked round to find the men, but discovered that there was not a sufficent number of rugby players to make up a full team. There was only one thing for it, therefore, and we set about it immediately. Games were arranged, and teams played in relays for most of us could not stand the pace. The eventful day arrived, and we clambered into motor lorries and set out for Lillers full of hope. Some of the members of the Battalion team had never played rugby before and, when they lined up against their opponents, found to their horror that the so called medium team included five internationals. The inevitable happened. The whistle blew and in a flash our opponents had scored. The game, of course, was hopeless from the start, and the score against us went up rapidly to twenty one points. However, just before the end Jones vowed he would score once, even if he died in the attempt and he did indeed score. He knocked over about half a dozen of his opponents in his rush, but he scored, and we accordingly came away feeling wonderfully cheered.

We had our humorous moments in the billets, and we were once very much amused when Walker, one of my pals, received a parcel of books from a dear old lady who lived opposite to him at home. Her intentions were obviously of the best, and it was clear that she wanted to provide some diversion to take 'Tommy's' mind off the horrors of war. Her selection of books, however, was somewhat unfortunate as we found that the parcel contained copies of 'Horners Penny Stories' and 'Home Chat'. There was plenty of home chat that night, for we pulled Walker's leg unmercifully, and I fear that he was not quite as grateful to the old dame as he might have been.

We were very much troubled by wasps, for they seemed to be everywhere. We put up with this annoyance for some time, but when they began to settle on our bread and jam in groups of four or five as we were actually putting it into our mouths, we decided to put a stop to their antics. We scrounged around to find their nest, and eventually ran them to earth in a lane at the rear of the billet. We tried to get near, but very soon there were swarms of them about our faces, and we had to beat a quick and undignified retreat. At last someone suggested smoke helmets. These we donned and, being protected from attack, we calmly placed burning straw over the nest and smoked them out, and from then onwards were able to eat in peace.

5 The Battle of Loos

Our rest and training came to an end at last, and on 21 September 1915 we left Lespesse in full fighting order complete with full packs etc. 'D' Company led the Battalion, and after marching for some time we arrived at the village of La Pugnoi. We were taken into a wood in order to be out of observation of enemy aircraft. There we had to wait before going into the impending battle for Loos. The guns were already blazing away in the preliminary stages of the attack. As we were to be there for the night in the open air, we set about making ourselves as comfortable as possible by rigging up some bivouacs with our ground sheets and, with the aid of billhooks which had been served out for the purpose of clearing away enemy barbed wire, we cleared away the brushwood as much as possible. I endeavoured to get some sleep at last, but it was a bitterly cold night and I was very glad to get up at 6.30am when the pipers played reveille.

We were 'standing by' all day and at night made a fire and sat round for a singsong. We spent another night in the wood, and the next day it began to rain so that we sat down on the ground with water running off our waterproof sheets. At 9pm the Battalion fell in and, half an hour later, we marched off towards the firing line. The rain was falling the whole time, and we were thoroughly wet through and felt utterly miserable.

Every wood that we passed was filled with troops, and after marching for about eight miles we arrived at Verquin and turned into an open field behind the stack of a colliery, where tea was served out to us and we were told to turn in for the night. 'Turn in' sounded good, but in fact there was not a scrap of cover anywhere, and the ground was thoroughly soaked by the rain. There was nothing for it, therefore, so I simply laid my ground sheet on the mud and, with my greatcoat over me, settled for a rest. During the night the rain pelted down incessantly so that I got absolutely wet through. We spent the next day in the field while the rain was still streaming down, so I rigged up a small

27

'bivvy' as a shelter. When everything was complete a member of the Signal Corps came along and informed me that the 'bivvy' had been fixed to a wire connected with one of the big guns, so it had to be dismantled.

The scheme of the forthcoming battle was outlined to us by our 'Skipper' Captain Anderson and, more particularly, the part that we were to play in it. At 9.30pm the Battalion moved off ready for the fray. We arrived at Vermelles and entered the trenches. The water in places was more than a foot deep, our boots soon filled up and we became plastered all over with thick oozy mud. After what seemed an endless journey we arrived some time after midnight at the section of trench in which it was intended we should spend the night.

Six of us, including myself, were Company bombers and we were issued with eight cricket ball bombs which were carried in pockets in an apron strapped round our kilt. These bombs had a detonator jutting out of the top covered with a piece of sticking plaster. On our wrist a band was worn, to which was attached the striking part of a box of matches, and we were also provided with matches. The procedure was as follows—to take the bomb from the pocket of the kilt apron, tear off the sticking plaster on the detonator, strike a match on the wristband and light the charge, hold the bomb for three or four seconds, then throw as far as possible. I do not know what genius devised this bomb with its farcical method of ignition, but I am very doubtful whether he ever spent a night in the pouring rain and tried to strike a match on his wristband, since even dampness put the striking band out of action. However, I have no doubt that he must have received some sort of reward for his services to the nation!

I have a further criticism to make; when one 'belly flopped' these eight bombs strung over one's kilt caused considerable pain in our most sensitive parts, and when we were wearing gas masks our eyes watered so much that we could not see out of the goggles. Of course one must be fair, and the underlying idea might have been that the enemy would have been so intrigued by our antics that he would have forgotten to fire.

But to continue the saga. We were all crowded together in a narrow trench and could not sit down, let alone lie down, for a rest. Rather than remain, therefore, in this very uncomfortable position all night, we clambered over the parapet, and lay down in the open on the ground behind. We had to hand in our overcoats before leaving Verquin and, as the rain was still falling, the cold was intense, so I lay down on the sodden ground wearing all my equipment, stretched my ground sheet over myself, and tried very ineffectively to keep out the rain. The famous cricket ball bombs became useless before ever we started into action. I was able to get about an hour's fitful sleep, and at 4.30am we again took up our positions in the trench. The artillery recommenced their bombardment, and very soon there was an intense cannonade going on all along the sector. Two hours after and just as it was getting light we had orders to put on our gas masks as the British were beginning to put over poison gas. The gas was invisible and was carried by the wind towards the German trenches. At one period, however, the wind veered round, and our own fellows were gassed in consequence. They came streaming past us with ghastly yellow faces from the effect of the gas, and the buttons on their tunics had been changed to a green colour.

Our starting–off point was a reserve trench about a quarter of a mile behind the front line and in front of the town of Loos. At 7.30am we received the order to go 'Over the Top' and from then onwards it was like hell let loose. Bullets came flying round us from all directions, machine guns spat out their endless stream of lead, and shells came whizzing with a sickening screech, and burst with a deafening roar. Everywhere around us showers of earth from the enemy's barrage were thrown up.

Our first casualty occured when we had gone forward about ten yards and was a member of my Platoon. He fell shot through the arm. We had received strict instructions before going into action that no–one was to stop to attend to the wounded, as these were to be left for the stretcher bearers. It was very distresssing to have to leave friends lying on the ground without being able to do something for them.

We walked over the ground from the reserve trench to the front line. At our second halt Savereux fell at my side with a wound in the back from shrapnel. We next ran into enfilading fire, and the place become very warm for the enemy's machine guns opened up on us. We had to advance over open country, and the Germans had us at their mercy. Just before the next halt, Walker, my own particular chum, fell shot through the left breast. He was next but one to me, but Fraser, who was next to him, was able to dress his wound before we received the order to go forward. It was hopeless, however, and he must have died soon after we left him. During the next rush we lost more men. There was a trench in front of us and we were ordered to get into it. I made a furious dive into the trench, and just missed empaling myself on the up–turned bayonet of a fellow who was sitting on the fire step. He was as much surprised at my arrival at I was to see his up–turned bayonet point. We now had time to take a breather in this trench, for there seemed to be deadlock ahead of us. The company in front had reached the enemy's barbed wire, but, owing to their depleted numbers and also due to the strength of the rifle fire from the German front line, they were unable to advance any further; consequently they had to lie down in front of the wire and await events. Our Company was then told to try and work round and attack the German trench from the left flank. There was a shallow sap running a little way from the left of the trench in which we had halted, and this ran out to a tree which stood to the left of the enemy's line in 'No Man's Land'. This tree had always been known amongst the troops as 'The Lone Tree'. Our object was to get across to this tree and to bomb down towards the centre of the enemy's lines, but owing to the rain that had fallen my bombs were useless as I was not able to light the fuse. At this moment and in these circumstances I definitely felt that I was 'Cannon Fodder'. We left the trench and made towards the Lone Tree with the bombers in front.

We rushed across without sustaining any casualties but the trench was very shallow and only afforded shelter in places, so we had to lie as close to the ground as possible with our heads down, and then to leap up and rush forward in groups. We had not gone far when we came under the fire, not only of the Germans, but also of our own men. In the excitement and confusion the regiment on our left flank mistook us for the enemy, and opened up on us with their machine guns. Holmes, the leading bomber, fell riddled with bullets through the head, and the rest of us had to crawl over his dead body. This was made more gruesome by the fact that we could see his brains spattered about him. We were all in a sorry plight because we could neither move forward nor backward, and we were being picked off one by one, for the little shelter that we had was not sufficient to protect us. Our numbers were too few to rush across the ground to the 'Lone Tree', for we would have been mown down before we got there. We were unable to get word back to our own men to stop firing, and so it seemed to be only a question of waiting for the end and trusting that it might be swift and painless. The tension was at its height when someone shouted 'Look at the Lone Tree'; they are taking prisoners'. I looked up and to my utter astonishment and, needless to say, my unspeakable relief, saw the Germans coming out of the trenches with their hands up to give themselves up as prisoners. This turn in events had been brought about by the Black Watch who had broken through the enemy's left flank, and seeing that our boys were held up had turned to their right and so cut off the retreat of the Germans on our immediate front. The enemy, seeing kilts in front and behind them, evidently deemed it expedient to throw up the sponge, and so filed out of their trenches.

We next saw some of the London Scottish coming towards us, and we had to wave a flag so that they might not mistake us for the enemy. The scene that followed was the most remarkable that I have ever witnessed. At one moment there was an intense and nerve shattering struggle with death screaming through the air. Then, as if with the wave of a magic wand, all was changed; all over 'No Man's Land' troops came out of trenches, or rose from the ground where they had just been lying. Prisoners were everywhere. There were about a thousand to fifteen hundred of them, and they were all marched off under escort, the Scottish taking charge of about five hundred. The Germans gave themselves up willingly and, except for the Officers, did not seem averse to their change of fortune.

The enemy had evacuated its front and second line of trenches, and this meant a cessation of hostilities for us, at least for the time being. We scrounged round the German trenches looking for souvenirs, and could smell traces of the gas that had been sent over earlier from our lines. We took over a trench, and had time to pull ourselves together, and to watch the bombardment.

Our casualties for the day had been heavy; close on three hundred out of five hundred and forty of the Scottish had fallen. In my own Company out of a hundred and one men, we had about forty five casualties.

Before going 'over the top' we had received orders that the water in our bottles was not to be touched until we had arrived at the German trenches. As we had reached our objective, therefore, we thought we were entitled to a drink; and so I had one, and not before it was necessary, because the reaction after the intense and nerve wracking excitement of the fight had left us with what seemed an almost unquenchable thirst. Food was not plentiful and all I had had to eat in twenty six hours was two and a half slices of bread and jam, a small piece of cheese and a handful of currants.

When darkness fell we moved forward, and then had to dig ourselves in. This consisted in scooping out, with the entrenching tools in our equipment, a trench sufficient to afford some cover. We had half finished this job when some chalk pits were discovered, and so we were taken to these. As we got to the edge of the pits the Germans opened fire on us and we had to descend very hurriedly. The pit was about forty feet deep with water at the bottom. The heavy rains had made the chalk very slippery with the result that most of us went down that slope in record time, and landed in a huddled heap at the bottom. A party of our machine gunners were left at the top to act as a guard. It was a bitterly cold night and sleep was impossible as we stood about in shivering groups. We were extremely glad, therefore, when we heard that we were to be relieved, especially since if a German counter attack came through in the night, the chalk pits would be a trap.

.Just as dawn was breaking we filed out of the chalk pit, and formed up on top. The German snipers were busy, and they 'bagged' two of our men, one of whom was quite close to me. We marched back to the reserve position and in doing so had to pass the ground over which the battle had raged the previous day. We had ample time to take everything in, and the sight was truly appalling. The dead were lying everywhere, some across the enemy's barbed wire. One could see limbs that been wrenched off by shells and some of the wounds were truly ghastly. Many of the wounded men were still lying out there, and some had done so for thirty six hours.

We were thoroughly exhausted, but cheered by the prospect of a rest. We were doomed to disappointment, however, for we had to take up another position in an evacuated German trench. The parapet was very low having been battered down by gunfire, and anyone passing along the trench came under the observation of the enemy; consequently we were shelled practically all day. A German counter attack was in progress to our left, so we had to move up to support the 3rd Brigade which lay in front of the little village of Hulloch. We thought we were to be in it again, for we had to go out and finish digging a trench commenced by other troops. We were informed that we would have to remain there for the next twenty four hours, so we had to work like mad in order to have sufficient cover by the time dawn broke. Bullets occasionally flew round us and two of the previous party had been hit working in that trench, so we stuck to our job all the harder. The want of sleep was beginning to tell on us all, for we had roughly had only about three hours sleep for three whole days. The digging was extremely hard work as the material to be dug out was chalk. Tea was brought up to us by a fatigue party, and it certainly tasted good. There were a great number of bombs lying about that had been left by the Germans. These had a string through the handle which, when pulled, exploded the bomb. None of these did in fact go off, although there was always the possibility that at any moment someone would trip over a string, or that a pick or shovel would catch in one and so set off the bomb.

It is as well to point out that I was still carrying the wretched and now useless cricket ball bombs in my kilt apron!

We worked until four thirty the next morning and then disappeared below the ground in the trench we had dug. A few shells and stray bullets came over us without serious results. We had to lie low during the day as we had instructions that we were not to allow ourselves to be seen. This injunction was hardly necessary, though, for during the afternoon there was a heavy bombardment, and the Germans enfiladed our trench, so that we were mighty glad to lie low. One shell blew in the traverse about

33

three yards from where I was sitting, but luckily I escaped injury. We were relieved that night by the South Wales Border-ers, and retired across the open to a trench lying in front of a farm known as 'La Rutoire Farm'. I turned in for a rest, but it was bitterly cold since our overcoats had been taken from us before going into action, though we had been allowed to retain our cardigans. These had been strapped on our belts at the back, but mine had become dislodged and I had lost it. I bitterly regretted its loss for without an overcoat I could not sleep for the cold. Corporal Campbell had been able to scrounge a German overcoat, so he let me have his ground sheet but this proved a poor substitute for a woollen cardigan.

The next day during a lull in the shelling, a couple of us got out of the trench and went over the ground of the recent action in an attempt to find the body of our pal Johnny Walker. After a considerable search we found him at last, and so knew for certain his ultimate end. He had been shot in the left breast very close to the heart, and must have died almost instantly. He lay there looking perfectly peaceful. In life Johnny had been a good look-ing boy with a bright expression and a merry twinkle in his eye, and even in death he looked serene.

He lay in a perfectly natural attitude as though he was just having a rest, and with his delicate hands and skin he looked like a figure carved in marble. Johnny was my personal friend, we had joined up together and from that day were practically inseparable. We shared everything, our joys and even our sorrows. As I gazed at him lying at my feet with that peaceful carefree expression on his face, I could hardly realise that he had left me for good and that I should never hear his merry chatter again, but that telltale hole over the heart brought back the grim reality. As time passed and the war lingered on I was to make other friends, but my heart still goes back to Johnny, and to this day I can still see him as he lay on that fateful battlefield at Loos, though the memory lingers on as a vision of peace.

Many years afterwards I went back to France and stood by his grave in the cemetery of the little village of Phylosofe, near Vermelles.

During a lull in the firing a battery of the Royal Horse Artillery went at a gallop along the Hulloch Road and when near the village of Loos pulled off the road, swung round the guns and began firing point blank at the enemy. Unfortunately, the Germans returned the fire and the whole battery was wiped out.

The shelling over our trench became very heavy in the afternoon, and we were peppered with high explosives and poison gas shells. When darkness fell I was sent out with two others to collect picks and shovels. We staggered along like three inebriates through the driving rain and thick mud on our quest. It was pitch dark and we could hardly see in front of us. We were not able to find the picks and shovels we were sent out for, but could not return without them. Providentially we stumbled across a dump which proved to be a stroke of luck for, on closer inspection, we found that the pile contained picks and shovels. They were not ours, but we refrained from asking questions, and stealthily helped ourselves. When I got back I was thoroughly wet through, so I stumbled around and eventually found a dugout occupied by two fellows of the Gloucestershire Regiment where I intended to turn in for a sleep. My kilt and tunic were sodden, and as I was thoroughly chilled to the bone I enjoyed very little sleep.

The next day, 29 September, we left the trenches for a brief rest and marched off at midnight and, after a short halt at Mazingarbe, during which we happened upon a store of biscuits and jam of which we speedily took advantage, we proceeded on our way until we arrived at La Brebis. The pipers met us on the way down and though we were weary and spent, it was marvellous how the skirl of the pipes put new life into us, and gave us just that little extra strength to get to our destination. When we got to La Brebis my Platoon was put into a room in an unoccupied house, and there we found a draft of new fellows who had just arrived from Rouen. Fifteen of us were put into two small rooms and we drew blankets and tea. Oh that tea! How delightful it tasted, and oh the gurgles of delight as it slipped down our parched and aching throats.

The room was certainly small, but it looked like Buckingham Palace to me then.

The Battalion that relieved us at the chalk pits was a battalion of the 21st Division. They had made a long march to the battlefield and had not been under fire before. On the march up their transport had been knocked to pieces and when the troops arrived they were tired and hungry with even their water bottles empty. As soon as they were down in the chalk pit they immediately took off their boots and equipment.

We heard later that the Germans had counter attacked, and caught the battalion unprepared, so that they suffered many casualties. It seemed heartless to send them in without a sprinkling of 'old hands' to act as a steadying influence, rather than treat them as 'Cannon Fodder'.

6 The Battle of Hulloch

After a good night's rest, we rose like giants refreshed, and spent the morning in endeavouring to clean off the mud which was caked all over us. This was by no means an easy task, for the mud was stuck to the hair on our legs, head and skins and, furthermore, was plastered thickly between the pleats of our kilts. However, we made ourselves fairly presentable by the time the Battalion moved off at 11.30am. We at length arrived at Noeux les Mines, and there were billeted in the environs of a coal mine. There was no grumbling this time, however, for the shed in which we were put was a palace compared with the trenches and, to crown it, there was an estaminet not twenty yards away. There we speedily adjourned, and were very soon indulging in egg omelettes. After this the parcel post which had been kept back while we had been in the trenches was delivered to us, so we started into the parcels straightaway.

We turned in to sleep fairly early, and although it was perishingly cold outside, we managed to keep fairly warm in our little wooden hut. The next day we spent in a further clean–up and those of us who were bombers had to hand in our bombs, but I had none to give up. Of course this was not considered strange, because officially I had exploded them in action. The truth, however, was that I had arranged to lose them. For days I had carried those infernal engines of destruction strapped to my stomach. They had been of no use to me, because I could not ignite them; furthermore, they were heavy, and a source of great discomfort to me, since if I crawled into a small hole in a trench for a sleep, there were those confounded bombs pressing into my stomach, so that every day in every way I had occasion to wish those bombs anywhere but slung round my anatomy. When the time came, therefore, to leave the trenches, I felt that the proper place for them was a trench, and accordingly at the dead of night those bombs and I parted company, and if I did not actually come away with a light heart, I felt a great load off my stomach.

After a stay of five days at Noeux les Mines, we again went back to the village of Vermelles, and set off to take up a position in a trench in advance of our old front line. We did not reach there until 2am, as our guide lost his way. The trench was very shallow so for our own safety we set about making it deeper. After this I was just preparing to get a little sleep, having done an hour's trench guard, when we received the order to 'stand to' with fixed bayonets, and at 4.30am we all had to leave the trench. Then followed another wearisome tramp until we arrived at the third line of trenches at 7am. In the afternoon another fellow and I were detailed to draw water for the Platoon. This was obtained from a well which had been dug by the Germans when they had occupied the trench. Whilst drawing the water, a high explosive shell came over and a piece hit me on the knee; luckily, however, it only drew blood.

The next day was a fairly light one for trench life. Sometime after dark a party of us sallied forth with rifles, picks and shovels to a position in advance of the Front line and in 'No Man's Land', and there we commenced to dig a new trench. On the way up we had to pass a sunken road, and this was strewn thickly with dead bodies. This was far from cheering and we anticipated a fairly warm time. While we were digging, however, we could hear the Germans talking a little way off. They were evidently out digging too, and so would not be likely to fire on us. Still, for all that there was quite an eerie atmosphere around and we dug hard to get a parapet in front of us, in case of trouble. At 3am we knocked off and, after 'B' Company had come up to hold the position for the night, we moved off. There was some delay on the way back, and we stood in the open expecting machine guns to open up on us at any moment. However, fortune favoured us and we eventually got back to our own trench at 5 a.m.

The next day the Germans gave it to us good and plenty for they bombarded us heavily, and our artillery returned with interest. About 1pm they bombarded us in earnest, preparatory to an attack. The bursting of high explosive shells and shrapnel was appalling, and no matter which way we turned we seemed to run into bursting shells. The only thing to do was to crouch down at the bottom of the trench and with palpitating hearts to wait and hope for the best. In the midst of this inferno we received an order to 'Stand to' on the firestep. This meant that German infantry were expected to come over in their hordes at any moment. Another fellow and I received orders from Captain Anderson to go back to Company HQ to bring up ammunition. To do this we had to go down the communication trench and, as this ran at right angles to the German line, there was no parapet to stop the shells and pieces of flying iron. How we got down there unharmed I do not know, but one thing I feel certain of is that we must have covered the distance in something like record time. When I reached Company HQ I grabbed as many bandoliers of ammunition as I could carry, and then sprinted back along the communication trench with the shells still bursting around me. When we got back the ammunition was distributed to the Company, and soon afterwards the Germans came over. Fortunately for us they were not on our immediate front; they came over against the 3rd Brigade, who were on our extreme right, but were driven back. While the attack was in progress the enemy kept up a heavy bombardment on our trench to make us keep our heads down, but at 5pm, to our intense relief, the enemy's fire slackened.

When darkness fell I went with a party to the 'Lone Tree' to draw rations for the Company. We had to cross open country and after the late 'shemozzle' expected a warm reception. We found the Battalion cookers at the tree, and I was given a tin of army biscuits to carry back. The 'Lone Tree' was the assembly point for the wounded, and all around on the grass there were dozens of wounded on stretchers waiting to be taken down by the ambulance column. This tree was a favourite for the German artillery and I could never understand why the wounded, transport, cookers and ambulances were allowed to congregate in this area. Apparently somebody later recognised the danger and the tree was felled. A piece of this tree with a bullet embodied in it is in my possession.

On our return to the trench the Company moved off to relieve 'C' Company in the support trench. I had to carry a petrol can of water for the Platoon, of course in addition to my rifle and equipment. The trench was long and narrow with wire catching one's head and feet, so that we arrived at our position thoroughly tired out. We were immediately told to get busy digging out the trench, but as far as I was concerned this was an impossibility for I was absolutely whacked. I had a short 'snooze' and then went on trench guard. The next day was fairly quiet as we were only shelled at intervals. After dark we made the trench deeper, and then I turned in for a short rest, but at 1am I was routed out and sent with two others to look for dead bodies. Our instructions were to take the identity discs or anything in the pockets that would lead to identity, and then to bury the body. A more gruesome job I have never struck, but we set off over the parapet on our cheerless task. We floundered about, but I am thankful to say did not come across any dead. Some of the Platoon were not so fortunate, however, since their beat included the sunken road where the dead were lying about in heaps.

Our small party then prepared to return, and then the trouble began, for we had lost our bearings. We came across another party of the Scottish in a similar predicament and while we were talking together a German shell landed about a yard from us. We all ducked, but by the greatest luck the shell proved to be a 'dud' and failed to explode on the soft ground. This did not calm our fears and we walked for a considerable distance till we heard a voice which turned out to be one of our own men, and much to our relief we again found ourselves at the trench from which we had set out earlier.

Shelling was continued on and off next day, and at 7pm I again had to go to the 'Lone Tree' for rations; this time I had to carry a sack of respirators for use against poisonous gas. On our way back there was a sudden burst of machine gun fire from our left, and the whole of us had to lie in the open flat on our stomachs to avoid the bullets which came flying over us. We carried the rations to the reserve trench, and waited for the rest of the Company to arrive. In the meantime I made myself as comfortable as possible in a dugout, but I had no sooner done so, however, when I had to bundle out again as our Platoon had to occupy another section of the trench. I eventually got down to rest in a German dugout about ten feet below ground level. The next day we moved to another German dugout which was about fifty feet long with proper sleeping accomodation and stoves for cooking; it was complete with wooden doors with blinds and, moreover, was well down in the earth. This feature appealed to us for the Germans shelled us pretty heavily at times. During the afternoon (11 October 1915) our Medical Officer was killed by a shell. On 12 October we had a very strenuous day in the way of trench fatigues. One little job alone, that of carrying bombs from Brigade HQ to 'C' Company in the front line, took four hours, On the way a shell struck the parapet just level with my head, but to my relief failed to explode.

When we arrived at the front line I again had a narrow shave, for the parapet above the fire trench came up to about my neck, so that my head was exposed. There was a whizz as a bullet from a sniper's rifle swept over; luckily I was stooping slightly at the time, and the bullet just missed me by inches.

At 10.30pm we again returned to the front line loaded with two days' rations, bombs and a box of smoke bombs. We set out over land, a thin line of figures stealthily wending our way nearer towards the German line. The enemy had searchlights out, but these were focused principally on aircraft. We arrived at our new postion at last, a narrow trench in advance of our own front line and in the village of Hulloch and of the German 'Hohenzollern Redoubt'. This latter was an almost impregnable trench system held by the Germans. During the night the shallowness of the trench was not such an inconvenience for under the cover of darkness we could stand up, but when dawn broke conditions changed and we had to sit on the bottom of the trench; otherwise we should have been seen by the Germans who were in their trenches barely two hundred yards away. We were to attack these trenches at 2pm (13 October) so that from dawn onwards we had to sit in a very cramped position for many hours, anxiously awaiting the order to go 'over the top'.

There was nothing to take one's mind off the future, and the suspense was terrible. The only distraction we had was the sound of artillery firing on the German trenches, but even then circumstances prevented us from having a look over to see the effect of the shelling. Everything depended on the enemy being unaware of the fact that we were in the trench, and thus of being taken by surprise when we leapt on him. The suspense was made even worse by the uncertainty as to the real state of affairs on our immediate front. This was increased by what we had been previously told. Some time before we had taken up our position our

Officer explained the general plan of attack, and told us exactly what we were expected to do. The aerial observation report was to the effect that the German trench in front of us was very weakly held. The artillery report was less reassuring, however. To the right of our front there was a thick wood, and in it a very small cottage. We were informed that it had not been possible to ascertain whether this was bristling with machine guns or not. Not to worry, however, because this doubt would be settled one way or the other as soon as the action started, and we appeared in the open. We were also given the assurance that at the first sight of machine guns our artillery would concentrate on the cottage. This sounded all very well, but I had heard this kind of talk before and, as much as I tried, I could not keep my mind off the thought of that cottage, and what it might contain.

I was with the rest of the Company bombers on the extreme right flank of the Company. Our leader was supplied with a red flag and, in the event of his being killed or wounded, the next bomber was to grab the flag and carry on. Our particular task was to get across to the German trenches, and to find a communication trench leading from it. In this we were to build a block by filling sandbags that we carried with us. The red flag was then to be hoisted an an indication to the artillery in the rear of our position, so that they could lift their barrage and fire on the Germans in the back areas. The plan was no doubt excellent in theory, but subsequent events did not go according to plan. In practice it was doomed to failure, for the flag made the carrier too conspicuous with the result that he was shot down immediately. Further events proved this opinion for, out of all the Company bombers, I was the only one who was unable to carry the flag, and the only one to come through alive and unwounded.

At 12.50pm our artillery began a concentrated bombardment on the enemy's trench immediately in front of us which, incidentally, advertised the fact that we were 'calling later'. This brought a furious reply from the Germans. Ten minutes later we all stood ready. Each of us had six smoke bombs; these we lit at intervals and threw out into 'No Man's Land'. The bombs emitted a cloud of dense smoke and a thick bank drifted towards the enemy lines. As soon as the Germans saw the smoke column they let fly with every gun they had, and very soon there was a terrific barrage of heavy shells bursting over our trench. Heavy rifle fire came from the Germans in the trench in front of us, and so proved that the report of their weak numbers was untrue; in fact there were more in that German trench than in our own, and we found out later that they were all Prussian Guards, about the hardest nuts that we could have come up against. The machine gun fire was terrific, so much so that we knew for certain that the little mystery cottage in the wood was bristling with them. True, our artillery got on to it, but this did not make the slightest impression, for the rate of intense machine gun fire never ceased all through the action.

Under cover of the smoke screen a party of bombers from the South Wales Borderers were sent along to reinforce us, and to hold the trench when we left to go into action. At 2pm we received the order to leave our haversacks and overcoats in the trench and to go 'over the top'. At the last moment the South Wales Borderers bombers were ordered to go over with us. This, however, they refused point blank to do, and allowed us to 'go over' alone.

The firing by this time had died down somewhat, for the Germans evidently thought that the smoke screen was merely bluff on our part.

We walked stealthily forward behind the smoke and, except for the occasional burst of rifle and machine gun fire, everything was going well till, unfortunately, a puff of wind blew away the smoke screeen in front of us, and we were spotted by the enemy. Then everything seemed to happen at once.

Machine guns and rifles poured a deadly hail of lead into our small party. I had not gone far, when I was hit in the thigh by a bullet; it felt like a kick from a mule, and the force of the blow knocked me completely head over heels. I pulled myself together, and then looked to my wound. Finding it only slight, the skin being merely grazed and slightly cut, I picked myself up and went forward. By this time I had lost touch with 'D' Company, so coming across 'A' Company who were going over on our right flank, I attached myself to them. On a closer inspection, I found that I had had a narrow escape. The bullet had hit the side of my water bottle, continued its course to the top, pierced the other side and, cut through five pleats of my kilt, grazed my side and eventually passed through the entrenching tool hanging on my belt at the back, and continued its career into space. The only injury that the bullet caused was the spilling of the water in the bottle—my sole supply for twenty four hours. In view of my escape I did not bother about this at the time, although later I regretted the loss bitterly when, in the heat of the battle, my parched throat ached longingly for a drink.

As soon as I joined 'A' Company, we could not move either way. The barbed wire in front was unbroken, so that we could not get through to the enemy trench, and a heavy barrage at the back of us prevented us from retiring. The heavy guns began to bombard us with shrapnel and, to put the finishing touch to our misery, our own guns, no doubt with a laudable intention of helping, began to shell the Germans in the trench in front of us. Unfortunately we were lying very close to the trench, and a great number of the shells fell short and caught our own men. Shells were also falling on the Hulloch Road to our right, sending the granite sets skywards. These came down again in a shower, inflicting many wounds. Seeing that we could not go forward I dug myself in with a German entrenching tool handed to me by Sergeant–Major Morton, since my own had a bullet hole through it and so was useless for digging purposes. I lay flat on the ground and, with my right hand, burrowed away till I had raised sufficient earth to cover my head and shoulders. I also made a mound at the side to protect myself from the enfilading machine gun fire to which we were being subjected. On returning the entrenching tool to the Sergeant–major I found that he was dead. This was indeed a shock. Corporal Campbell was lying in front of me slightly to the right. He raised his head a few inches to fire his rifle. His body quivered and he sank back with a bullet through the temple. Very soon I was lying there with dead all round me. The Germans from the trench in front of us were firing very low in order to catch us as we were lying down, and I could hear the bullets rustling through the grass on each side of me. Behind I could hear the groans of the wounded. Every now and then one of them called out 'Mother, Mother', and at times 'Scottish'. Someone called out for morphia tablets, but of course there were none available. Our advance had been checked, and we

44

survivors had to lie under hellish fire for four solid hours.

The longed for darkness came at last, and at 6.15pm the order was passed along that the rest of the Company were to retire sixty yards. This operation has to be carried out with great caution, for the Germans were sending up star shells making 'No Man's Land' pratically as clear as day. We were so near to them that any movement would betray our position out there in front of their barbed wire. I crawled back on my hands and knees, and whenever a star shell was sent up kept perfectly still until the last rays flickered and faded away. After some time I had covered the necessary distance. It was then found that the right section of the Scottish had lost touch with the rest of the Company. As I was the end man of the left half I was given orders to go out and endeavour to make contact with the Company. I crept off in the darkness and in a quiet voice called for the Scottish. I found them at last struggling along and pointed out the way to them. I returned to our new position, and then dug myself in and lay there awaiting events. Guards were set in case the Germans attempted to rush us in a counter attack. I am afraid we could have done nothing to stop them if they had decided to come over, for we were exceedingly few in number, and could have offered only very feeble resistance. From that point I remember nothing, as I fell right off to sleep.

I awoke at about 10pm to find a line of forms in front of me digging. I was very startled because I could not make out whether they were friend or foe. I dared not move for fear they were Germans, and so lay still hoping that someone would speak, and so betray their nationality. I was still undecided when a figure appeared out of the darkness at the back of me, and dropped at my side. This turned out to be one of our Officers, Major Low, who informed me that the line of figures were 'B' and 'C' Companies, who had come up about two hours previously to relieve us. I could have shouted with relief. I got up speedily and made my way back to where I thought our trench was, but I lost my bearings, and could not find the trench anywhere. I went on, however, and eventually out of the blue heard the ominous challenge 'Achtung'. I immediately flopped down and after a time got up and carefully walked away from what was obviously a German trench. I was thoroughly exhausted and eventually fell over into a trench by accident. As luck would have it, this was the one for which I was looking. I looked in vain for the haversack I had left there in the afternoon, but I found Fraser's pack and, as he had been wounded and I was bitterly cold, I took his overcoat to get a little warmth.

The remnants of the Company were then withdrawn to the third line of trenches, and there I was able to snatch a sorely needed sleep. At 3.15am we were aroused, and the whole Company moved up again to the support trench.

Our casualties had been heavy, and out of my Platoon (Number 13) which had gone into action twenty strong, only three of us were left. The whole Company had numbered seventy, and of these only twenty remained. The Brigade on 25 September (Loos) numbered five thousand, but after the ensuing battle of Hulloch ('Hohenzollern Redoubt') on 13 October, six hundred only remained.

We moved to another trench called 'Fence Alley' near the Rutoire Farm. We were all very jumpy and glad to get back to comparative safety. The Germans sent 'Coal boxes' over our trench; these were shells from very heavy guns. One of our Sergeants was killed by concussion alone, with not a mark on him.

About 6pm we left the trenches to go for a rest. We staggered along, and arrived at Sailly la Bourse, and as we dragged ourselves into the village 'C' Company sent up a cheer. Stew was served out to us and after a long rest we carried on until we got to Noeux les Mines. There we turned into a field for about an hour, and at midnight entrained at the station, and the delight at being pulled along in a train instead of having to continue on our tottering 'pins' was indescribable.

When the train stopped at Lillers we were all asleep, and had to be awakened by our Quarter Master Sergeant. We detrained and were guided to our billet. The journey from the station was very hard going, for the streets were made up of cobbles, and these very nearly put paid to our sore feet.

Our billet was a semi-built factory, and as a convalescent home for consumptives the building would have been admirable, for there were no windows. The boards on the floor had not been nailed down and there were ladders instead of staircases. Nevertheless, we were far from being in a critical mood and, with many grunts of satisfaction,

we climbed the ladders to the first loose floor and sunk down on the
boards for a rest.

7 Rest at Lillers

Our rest at Lillers was fairly uneventful, and we were allowed a moderately easy time. The deficiencies in our kit were made up, and those who required them had new tunics and boots served out.

The Battalion parcel post had been kept back while we had been in action, but this was now served out and amounted to seventy mail bags. I received thirteen parcels, and for days I hardly touched army rations. A new draft from Rouen was in the billet when we arrived from the trenches, and as they had been on short rations, the rest of us made a dump of unopened parcels on the floor and told the newcomers to sail into them. They thought we were the kindest fellows in the world, and never was a reputation so easily gained.

'It never rains but is pours', for I received in addition to the other parcels one sent from the Queen Alexandra Field Force Fund. I do not know how many times the selection committee of the Fund met before coming to the definite decision as to what the parcel should contain, but that their selection was good can be seen from the fact that each parcel contained:

Towel
Mittens
Writing Tablet
Laces
Muffler
Sleeping Helmet
Soap
Handkerchief
Box of Matches
Toilet Paper !!!

Everyone was sorely in need of a bath and, accordingly, arrangements were made for us at the local brewery. A couple of huge beer vats were filled with warm water from a hose, and six of us at a time bathed in each vat.

The billet was very draughty and cold, so one night we lit a fire in an old petrol can. We were comfortably settled round it when the owner of the factory in which we were billeted appeared in a tearing rage, accompanied by an interpreter. He objected to the fire, although we tried to convice him that everything would be all right. He went away, and later returned with one of our Officers. The latter sympathised with us, but told us to let the fire die down. This we did, but as occasionaly one of those seated round accidentally dropped a piece of wood on, the fire took quite a time to die down.

I received a telegram from home with regard to a Commission, and so set off to send a reply. I did not think this was going to present any difficulties, but I was to find out my mistake. I first went to our Signallers to find out about the censoring of my reply telegram. On their direction I proceeded to the French Post Office. There I obtained a form and was referred to Number 6 Clearing Hospital for censorship. On reporting there I was informed that the Town Major had to see it first. Back to the Town Major therefore I went. I found him to be a beaming French Officer who censored the telegram and wished me luck. I then had to return to the clearing hospital for the English censoring stamp to be affixed. Everything was now apparently in order, and I handed the telegram over the counter of the French Post Office.

Hallowe'en was celebrated in our billets, and during the morning we hauled barrels of beer up to the first floor. As there were no staircases this had to be done by ropes. At 3pm we sat down to a dinner of:

Soup
Roast Beef
Plum Duff

There was also whisky for those who were that way inclined. 'The Dining Hall' was not elaborate, with bare brick walls, no windows and huge gaps in the floor. Our table was made up with bricks and boards, and newspapers served as tablecloths. The floral decorations consisted of two woebegone–looking ferns. These were placed on centres of cut paper. The Officers were present and the Colonel made a short speech.

In Battalion orders there was a notice that any solicitors in the

Battalion should report to HQ. I accordingly went along, with visions of a 'cushy' job in the future; however, I found that I was required to appear at a court martial to defend a high ranking NCO of another regiment, who had been arrested for drunkenness while on duty in the trenches. Sergeant Pirrie of the Pioneer section and myself interviewed the accused NCO who admitted that he had no answer to the charge, so that our prospects of success were practically nil.

The Court Martial was held at the HQ of the Gloucester Regiment, and consisted of Major Sutherland (Black Watch attached to the Gloucesters), Captain Anderson (London Scottish), and a Captain of the Cameron Highlanders.

There were also fifteen other Officers present for instructional purposes. The guard at the door, seeing a private soldier, at first would not let me in, but as I was for the time–being solicitor for the defence he had to. The accused stood in the centre of the room with a guard with fixed bayonets. The trial lasted two hours; of course it was hopeless, and in the end the judgment of the court was reserved, and I returned to my billet. Four days later the verdict was announced and the accused was found guilty and was reduced in rank. All things considered he was extremely lucky, as the offence by a man of his rank was rightly thought to be a very serious one.

During our stay at Lillers, the Division was inspected by King George V and a party of us were chosen to represent the Company. Let me hasten to add that, personally, I think I was chosen on account of length of service, and not for personal smartness. The bagpipes sounded Revielle at 4am and we reluctantly turned out. It was very tantalising to hear those who were not going snugly tucked up in their blankets. To their jibes we retorted that the Battalion only preferred the smart–looking troops and that they had no use for 'washouts'. I would have given anything just then to have been a 'washout'. We cleaned rifles, boots and buttons and there was a considerable amount of wholehearted grousing about it. At 6am we paraded in the drizzling rain, but fortunately it was too dark for the Officers to make a close inspection. The Company joined the rest of the Battalion in the Rue de la Mère, and then marched off to the inspection ground at La Buissière, and were in position about three hours later.

After having trudged through the mud our cleaned boots looked a picture. The parade ground was situated in a valley with a road between the two slopes. The whole Division was present, and consisted of twelve thousand troops, together with artillery, machine guns and ambulances. It was an imposing sight, but the effect was somewhat marred by drizzling rain.

We shivered for about half an hour, and the King came along on horseback at the trot. I was in the last rank of the last Company of the last Battalion of the Brigade and saw practically nothing. We felt miserably cold, and did not fully appreciate the honour that had been bestowed on the Division. We learned later that after having trotted past us the King had been thrown from his horse.

8 No. 26 General Hospital

During the time that we were at Lillers, I developed impetigo which affected my hands and legs, and I paraded before the MO for treatment from time to time. I got worse and as I developed a temperature the MO Captain Patterson (who was acting for our own MO) marked me for hospital. On 9 November I went round to the dressing station with my rifle and kit. There I was bandaged and when an ambulance arrived an hour later I clambered in, together with another Scottish fellow. We were taken to the little village of Auchele, about four miles from Lillers, to a hospital in the Hôtel de Ville, where an MO examined us. Each of us was given a card with our name and particulars on it; mine was marked on the back with the words 'For Evacuation'. This sounded rather promising. We remained there for some time, and were then taken back again to Lillers to the First and Second West Riding Hospital. There we were again examined, and our rifles and equipment were taken from us. I was put into a marquee together with fourteen others. Each of us had a stretcher to sleep on, and glory of glories, four blankets.

The next day the MO ordered me to another tent, and I was carried on my stretcher and dumped in a tent all on my own. This did not look so promising, but I waited to see what turned up. After dinner I was rescued by an RAMC orderly who told me that there had been a mistake and that I was in the wrong tent. I was then moved again and put in with ten other patients. On 11 November I was sent to the Base. Those of us who could, walked to the train, while the other cases were taken by ambulance. We were put into a Red Cross train, with stretchers fixed up in the position usually occupied by the luggage racks. We steamed out of Merville to pick up more casualties; on the journey the French sentries presented arms as the Hospital train passed along.

We returned to Lillers and continued on to Etaples via Béthune and Abbeville, arriving at 2.30am. Motor ambulances met us and if the ambulance went to the right, it went to Number 26 General Hospital (the English Hospital); if it went to the left, it was going to the

Canadian Hospital, where the troops had a wonderful time and a sporting chance of getting home to Blighty. This is where my luck let me down for my ambulance turned right, and I landed in the English Hospital, with not much chance of getting home. After our particulars had been taken in the reception hut, I was sent off to Ward 32. On entering the hut a wonderful sight met my eyes, for behold there were beds with white sheets. A glorious wash in warm water followed, then clean shirt and night clothes, and then a nestle between the sheets. I could not sleep, everything seemed so strange.

Things looked up next day, especially in the food line, for breakfast consisted of porridge and tea. Our next hope rested on dinner. This exceeded our expectations, for lamb, peas and potatoes, and rice pudding rolled up. Supper was at 7pm and consisted of cocoa and bread and butter. At 8pm all lights were put out, and so came to an end a perfect day. The next morning at 4.30am I was awakened out of a glorious sleep and a basin of water was brought for us to wash with . I should have preferred to have had my morning wash later, say about 7.30am, for 4.30am was a bit of a shock. I was kept in bed, but was allowed to get up after four days. I was then given a Hospital suit and what a suit! The hue was Oxford blue, with white facings. Judging from the size of the particular suit that was handed to me it must have been intended for a Life Guardsman. I had to turn the trouser legs up till the turn–ups nearly reached my knees, so that the white facings were quite a spectacle. The bagginess allowed plenty of room for bending. There was one serious drawback and that was the entire absence of pockets. A flaring red necktie added quite a socialistic touch.

Life passed very peaceably and, compared with the trenches, was like living on another planet. We spent the time mostly in reading, and in indulging in endless arguments. I was detailed to clean the windows of the ward, but as my hands were swathed in bandages this would have been no easy job, so I paid a medical orderly to do it for me.

We had one patient in the ward who was brimful of cockney wit. He was waiting to have an operation, but did not know when. In the meantime he used to amuse us enormously by his antics. On one occasion he was performing a warlike dance in his long night shirt, when at that moment the door opened and two medical orderlies appeared in long white coats with a stretcher to take him off for his operation. When they saw him doing the Highland Fling they hesitated. The rest of us, of course, roared with laughter, but the performer misunderstood it as being due to his dancing prowess. After a time, however, he began to have his doubts and so looked round and, when he saw the two spectres in white, fell flat on the floor. He was returned sometime later on a stretcher, the operation having been successfully completed.

On one occasion an epidemic of diarrhoea swept through the hospital, and calls of nature became very pressing. Unfortunately, the latrines were about two hundred yards away, and this was too far in some cases. Luckily I was very little affected, but others were not so lucky and had to spend the night in the latrine, somewhat holding up the queue that was waiting outside.

After having been in hospital for about a month, I was considered fit enough to go to the convalescent camp. My uniform was handed back to me and when I saw it I very nearly had a fit, for it had been creased all over by the fumigation process. We were taken in an ambulance to a camp nearby. On arrival more particulars were taken, then I was put into Number 6 hut, where there were boards and trestles to sleep on with blankets, but no sheets. The era of peacefulness was quickly drawing to an end, much to my disappointment. My stay here was short and on the fourth day I set off with a party to Etaples station, where we entrained in cattle trucks—the gripping hand was again gradually closing in on us. We arrived at Rouen after having been in the trucks for about twenty one hours, and then marched up to the same camp outside the town in which I had spent some time on my first arrival in France.

I spent about five weeks at Rouen waiting to be included in the next draft that was to be sent to the 1st Battalion. There was the same camp routine, with the same monotonous parades on the cavalry parade ground. I also had to parade before the MO on numerous occasions, as I had developed laryngitis; despite this, however, I still had to appear on parade. The MO did not seem to do my throat any good, so I gave up going to him, and decided to let things take their own course. One evening I went to the cavalry hut (YMCA canteen). After a while, I went to the counter to get some refreshment. I gave my order in a hoarse croaking voice that was almost inaudible. One of the good lady helpers, a motherly dame, asked me what was the matter, and immediately insisted that I should sit with my head over a jug of steaming water. I tried to back out, but there was no escape, for she took no notice of my remark, but speedily went off and soon produced the necessary. There I sat, in view of the whole hut, under the gaze of curious onlookers, sniffing steam and I felt far from heroic. As soon as there was an opporutnity I made my exit, and took good care not to go into that hut again.

My first Christmas day (1915) on active service was spent in the camp. The helpers at the YMCA hut did their best to make it as much like Christmas for us as they could. A dinner was arranged and we helped by cutting up cake, buttering rolls, and by making ourselves generally useful. Christmas pudding graced the board at dinner.

In the afternoon we set the table and at 4.15pm there was a Fancy Dress tea. The hut was decorated with paper chains and lanterns, and Christmas trees with lighted candles adorned the tables. A concert followed with the Camp Commandant in the Chair. A parade of fancy dress competitors from all the Regiments came after and the London Scottish pulled off first, second and third prizes.

After an enjoyable evening we returned to our tents, and were soon asleep. Some time after midnight I was awakened from my slumbers by a great noise outside the tent. I found that the disturbance had been created by two members of the Scottish who had appeared at the Fancy Dress tea. Instead of coming straight back to the tent from the YMCA hut, they had gone on to the Sergeants' Mess, and from there to the Officers' Mess. As the whisky had been going round freely the two returning vagrants were decidedly 'oiled'. One of them had appeared in costume as the YMCA Pay Box, and would persist in trying to get through the narrow opening of the tent with the box-like contraption still round him. This was of course impossible, but in the middle of the skirmish the 'cashier in the pay box' fell with a mighty crash and the pay box collapsed. At last he fell into the tent, and at sundry intervals thereafter related to us the numbers of whiskies and beers he had imbibed. He was greatly perturbed by the fact that he had aroused us from sleep and would keep on apologising profusely. He next spent a long time trying to persuade us that he had not really awakened us at all, but that we had all awakened of our own accord. At last he went off to sleep with all his uniform on.

On 31 December we turned out of the tent to see the New Year in. We planted the Scottish flag and, forming ourselves in a ring around it, were soon swaying to the strains of Auld Lang Syne. After the passing of the old year we gripped the flag and marched up and down singing the 'Hodden Grey', the Regimental Song of the 1st London Scottish.

1916

9 Return to Battalion—Leaving 1st Division

The period of waiting at Rouen came to an end on 19 January 1916, and, after having been served out with fur coats, gas helmets and ammunition, we set off in the afternoon for the station. My attack of laryngitis was still severe, and the only way I could attract peoples' attention was by first whistling, and then croaking out in a hoarse whisper. We entrained at 5.30pm.

No–one was allowed to leave the train at the various halts, and to prevent this guards were stationed on the ballast. Our progress was exceedingly slow, as there had been a goods train smash in front. We arrived next day at Lillers, and then marched off to Burbure, a village about two miles away. I went along to Number 13 Platoon billet which I found to be a room in an estaminet. The Platoon were out on a Guard of Honour to General Joffre and did not return until the evening. There were very few of the old faces left and the Platoon practically consisted of new fellows who had come up in drafts. At first I felt quite a stranger and experienced a great feeling of loneliness. This passed, however, as I began to know the new fellows. The Battalion remained at Burbure just on three weeks. My throat had not improved, and I felt far from fit, so after a few days days I went to see the MO who marked me for 'light duty'.

Towards the end of our stay at Burbure there were rumours that the Battalion was to leave the 1st Division, and on 8 February these rumours were confirmed, for we had to pack up ready to go off to an unknown destination.

At midday the Company fell in, in full pack and equipment, complete with tin helmets and fur (sheepskin) coats. We joined the rest of the Battalion on the village green, where we were ordered to fix bayonets—not an easy job in the slippery mud. The GOC General Rawlinson arrived, and we presented arms. He made a short speech of farewell, and the pipers played 'The General Salute'. I do not remember much of the General's speech, but he seemed to be awfully earnest about it and certainly took everything very seriously. He wound up his remarks by saying that 'we're all one in our great task to kill the Boche! kill the Boche!! kill the Boche!!!'. At that moment I must confess that my feelings were not quite so bloodthirsty as the General's.

The Battalion then marched off to Lillers station. The Pipes of the Black Watch and Brass Bands, together with the Divisional Band, headed our column and as we passed the billets of the Cameron Highlanders on our way they all turned out and lustily cheered us. At Lillers we clambered into cattle wagons, and later steamed out and so left Lillers and the 1st Division.

10 The 56th Division

We spent the greater part of the day in the train, and late at night alighted at Pont Remy. When the cookers had been unloaded from the train tea was made for us, after which we set off in the darkness for a six mile tramp through a snowstorm to Helencourt. We fondly imagined that this was our destination, but no, we toiled on and eventually halted at the village of Mirlemont. The Battalion was billeted in a shed adjoining a factory. There were no blankets, so I made the best of it with my overcoat and fur (sheepskin) coat. I had been very seedy all day, and so being thoroughly worn out fell asleep.

We moved on again next morning, and after marching for four miles came to Forceville, a village about fifty miles behind the firing line. Two Companies were quartered in Forceville ('C' and 'D') and 'A' and 'B' Companies were stationed at Neuville, a village about a mile away. 'D' Company was put in the basement of a school, but we had just made ourselves comfortable when we were moved to another billet. This was a loft over a barn, and we had to go up a ladder to get to our new quarters. Our blankets failed to turn up, so we had to spend another night without them. The snow lay thick outside, and the cold inside was intense. Later the billet was condemned by the Medical Officer for out of the twenty four occupants, seven were marked unfit, one of whom had to be sent to hospital. We were shifted, therefore, to new quarters. A few days after, our new billet was wanted for a Company canteen, so we were put out, and again shifted to other quarters in a barn; it was extremely draughty and not at all to our liking. One of the platoon members found a private billet and invited me to go along to it, an offer which I gladly accepted. I found the new quarters to be the outhouse of a cottage, and there were six altogether in it. The good lady of the cottage supplied us with straw mattresses and she allowed us to sit in the kitchen at night, so that 'everything in the garden was lovely'.

We spent about eighteen days at Forceville and, during part of the time, experienced very severe weather. One morning on getting up, we found our mattresses covered with snow, and our boots were frozen stiff like iron. We took the precaution afterwards of leaving our boots by the fire in the kitchen at night.

The area around us had been allocated to a new Territorial Divison, the 56th. We were the first Battalion to arrive, as the bulk of the Division had not left England. There was at that time no proper organisation. We had no Supply Column or Field Hospital, but fortunately our blankets turned up at last.

The time was spent in the usual drilling, round the surrounding country. There was a château near our billets belonging to the Comte de Forceville, and there we had baths in the scullery. By 27 February the brains of the divisional staff had evidently had time to function, for they discovered that the Battalion was in the wrong billeting area, so we received orders to move to another area about thirty miles or so away. We sallied forth, therefore, with packs feeling as heavy as lead and, having gone about fifteen miles, arrived at a village called Bouchon. We had started at 8.45am, and arrived at 3.30pm, with only a halt of twenty minutes at midday. My Platoon was put into a billet that only had two walls and a part of a third, and a couple of horses were also put with us. I later moved my tackle to Number 14 Platoon billet. We had no blankets and it was freezing hard. The fellow next to me had an attack of influenza and gave me the creeps all night with his shivering and moaning. We were up early next morning ready to move on again, but as so many men of the Brigade had fallen out the previous day, the move was postponed.

The next day I was detailed with a party to go to Longpré, about four miles off, where we reported to the Officer in charge of the Divisional Supply Column, and were temporarily attached to the Army Supply Column for the purpose of loading lorries. This was a pleasant little interlude, and lasted for five days. Our job consisted principally of going out to Longpré station in a lorry to pick up stores from the Supply train, and of going to the village of Domart about twelve miles away, and there unloading maize, bread, meat etc. Needless to say, as we were with the ASC, rations were good compared with those issued to the Infantry, and we fed like fighting cocks. This of course was too good to last, and we had orders to return to the Battalion, so on 5 March we were taken back to Bouchon on a motor lorry.

On 11 March we marched to Flixecourt, and there carried out a practice attack ending with a grand march past General Sir Douglas

Haig and Field Marshal Foch. The next day we left Bouchon for Douilens about twenty miles away and I felt 'all in' when we reached our destination. The march had been a very gruelling one, for we were the last Regiment in the column; consequently the length of our halts was practically halved. About a hundred fellows fell out, and these were picked up by ambulances. There was a twenty minute halt at midday, but no dinner, and our 'sails' were flapping pretty freely by the time we staggered into Doullens.

We were billeted in a factory, where the door leading to the engine room was marked 'Défense D'Entrer'. The engine room suggested warmth, so, emulating the great Nelson, we turned a blind eye to the notice and went in, and later laid down there for a sleep. Early next morning a Frenchman appeared, and shouted out to us to clear out. Although most of us were awake no–one answered for fear that he would want us to clear out straightaway. As his shouting had no effect, he resorted to other measures. He disappeared, and very soon after the whole room was flooded with steam from the engine. We stuck it out, and got up in our own time. Later on we had to give up our little warm corner, and go to other quarters. Three days afterwards we moved on again and after another agonising march arrived at the little village of Villers sur Simon fifteen miles away. We struck quite a good billet, for we were put into a large attic over a farmhouse. The floor was of brick, but was somewhat insecure and one of the company nearly fell through.

11 Villers sur Simon

The Battalion now formed part of the 168th Brigade which consisted of The Royal Fusiliers, The Rangers, The Kensingtons and The London Scottish.

The Scottish were the only unit yet arrived at the training and concentration area. We stayed at Villers for seven weeks and, considering that there was a war on, had quite a good time.

The Halley Claymore Competition for the best drilled Company was held and, to everyone's astonishment, 'D' Company came in a good second to 'C', for we only lost first place by one point; there were football matches and concerts arranged by the various companies. We also held a horse race, the transport fellows turned out arrayed as jockeys, and took bets on the field. The race was a great success and was won by Billy, one of the pack animals. He was ridden by a youngster, and when the horse got to the winning post it refused to stop, dashed off the field and away through the village, and was only brought to a standstill when it got to its stable.

Our Padre went on leave, and so in place of his sermon on Sunday, the Colonel read the Army Act to us. I made a special note of the offences for which we could be shot—and there seemed to be quite a number!

On 25 April 1916 there was a Brigade route march. We started off full of spirit on a fifteen mile march, but it was a sweltering hot day and the sun pouring down on our steel helmets soon began to have its effect. Soon fellows began to drop like flies, and the Officers allowed their packs to be carried on their chargers. The Brigadier spotted this, and gave orders that the packs were to be given back to their owners. We struggled on with ambulances following us up. Some of the marchers fell out with sunstroke, and I noticed many with blood oozing from their boots, and in a state of utter exhaustion. We were very nearly 'all out', but made up our minds that at any rate the Scottish were not going to give the Brigadier the satisfaction of seeing that he had marched us to a standstill. When we saw him, therefore, at the crossroads (on his horse!) watching us as we passed we pushed out our chests and tried to look as if we were enjoying it. When at last I got back to my billet I simply sank down on the ground, and for a time had not sufficient strength to rise, nor even to remove my equipment. When eventually I was able to stand up, my feet felt as though they were being pressed onto a bed of needles. The Scottish had the fewest number to fall out in the whole Brigade. We learned later that three fellows in the rest of the Brigade had died from exhaustion, as a result of a *practice* march.

One of the Company cooks was sent to a neighbouring village to cook for a party of the Scottish who were there on a bombing course. Lance Corporal Arnot, who was in charge of 'D' Company cooker, asked me therefore, if I would temporarily fill the vacancy. I scented that there might be more behind this offer than appeared at the first blush, because I used always to pull their legs unmercifully, telling them that they had a 'cushy job', and that it was not soldiering at all. Arnot told me later that that was the reason, and he wanted me to have an opportunity of finding out for myself that it was not so 'cushy' as I thought. I joined the cooks therefore, temporarily, and remained for good. The cooks for the Company numbered four. Later Arnot went home to England and so I was officially appointed a cook. I had not the faintest idea about cooking, but ignorance seemed to be the only qualification for a job in the army!

I shifted my tackle to the cooks' billet which was a stable they had cleaned out, and from what they told me it needed it badly, for there was about two feet of manure on the floor. The Cooker (to give its official name 'Field Kitchen') stood in the open in a field at the back, and I found to my cost later, that work on it was mighty uncomfortable when the rain pelted down.

There was a well in the yard from which we used to draw the water for cooking. One evening I let down the bucket and began to pull it up again, but it felt heavier than usual, and when it appeared at the top, I saw to my surprise two German helmets. We did not enjoy our tea in the least that night and, as the next well was some way off, we kept our mouths shut about the find, and carried on using this same well.

It was our custom to bank up the fire in the cooker overnight, so that it would be alight in the morning. On various occasions we found that the fire was out and could not discover the reason. One night, however, I happened to go out to the cooker just in time to see the old boy who lived in the house close by walking off with a shovel full of burning embers from our fire. We followed him to the house, and had a few things to say to him.

There was some very tempting looking rhubarb growing in the field at the back. The old fellow was always away all day, so I went in and helped myself. I came away with an armful and, to my surprise, ran full tilt into the 'boss', who had come back earlier than usual. I decided to take the bull by the horns and went straight up to him and asked if I might have some rhubarb. He looked rather old fashioned at me, but nevertheless said 'yes'. Later his son, a boy about fourteen, saw the rhubarb cooking, and said his father wanted to know where we had got it. I told him to tell his father that we had got the rhubarb from the same place as he got the coal, and that closed the matter.

A word should be said about this boy, because although he did not realise it, he was an unfailing source of amusement to us. He rejoiced in the name of 'Urinoir'—and I need hardly add that we always called him 'Urinal'. He obviously did not understand what it meant, because he took this as a great compliment, and his face would beam with pleasure when we addressed him so. I think, too, that we brought a little happiness into his young life, at least I hope so. He lived alone with his father and consequently yearned for companionship. He spent every available moment with us. At times he would do anything for us, and then something we did would rattle his temper, and he would become as obstinate as a mule. He was in one of these moods one day, when we asked for permission to use a brick oven that was in an outhouse. His father was away, and Urinoir refused point blank to let us use it. He stood like Ajax defying the lightning with his arms stretched out across the doorway. We were determined to use that oven though so we caught hold of him, ran him indoors and locked him in the kitchen. Meanwhile we 'borrowed' his father's wood and proceeded to light a fire in the oven. All the time there were murderous threats and screams issuing from the kitchen. At length when the dinner was ready, we released Urinoir and he left us severely alone for the rest of the day.

When he was particularly annoyed with us he would come up to the door of the stable in which we were billeted and would set up a terrific kicking and then run off. He did this once too often though, for we decided to lay a trap for him. We took no notice and so lulled him into a sense of security. As nothing seemed to happen, therefore, he sat on the edge of a horse trough close by the door, and kept up a continuous volley of kicks. Then suddenly Clark, a transport fellow who was billeted with us, quickly threw open the door and with his foot tilted poor Urinoir backwards into the horse trough. It was the neatest piece of work I ever saw. Urinoir clambered out and ran off dripping from head to foot, and we did not see him for the rest of the day. He used to go out practically every day into the fields with his father, and once I thought I would give him a little surprise. There were some cows in a shed in the yard, so I went in, untied one, and solemnly walked it into the house. I took it through the front door and into the kitchen where I left it. Some time after, Urinoir returned alone and, as he came in the big gates of the yard, his face was wreathed in smiles. We took no notice, but waited for the fun to begin. Poor Urinoir had the shock of his life when he got indoors. He rushed out again, shouting at the top of his voice that his father would kill him. His distress was obviously so genuine that I decided to get the cow out before the 'ogre' returned, for we did not want to be the cause of Urinoir getting a hiding. But getting that cow out was a tough proposition. It went in all right, but I had a terrible job getting it out again. I tried to turn that animal round, but it just could not be done. Once or twice its horns very nearly went through the glass windows. At length in sheer desperation, I caught hold of its horns and gingerly steered it backwards. I got it into the yard and took it back to the shed. My relief, however, was nothing compared with the relief of Urinoir when he saw the cow back in its shed again.

Now we had always seen Urinoir in shabby farm clothes and our surprise therefore knew no bounds when, on Easter Sunday morning, we saw him sally forth from the house on the way to early Mass, resplendent in new 'togs', and to crown it all a straw boater. The hat was too much for us. Poor Urinoir was terribly self conscious, and we could see that he was very doubtful as to what reception he was going to get. Instead of coming to us, therefore, as he usually did, he walked very gingerly round the walls of the yard, trying to attract as little attention as possible. He had just got to the yard gates, and was nearly out of range, when we all let fly at him with a volley of potatoes. One potato got him and hit the straw hat, sending it flying into the road. He simply picked it up and ran. When he returned later from Mass it was noticeable that he held his straw hat under his arm. He was a game kid really, and nothing seemed to damp his ardour. Of course we were not always worrying the life out of him; many a time we gave him a feed—and, poor kid, looked as if he needed it. It was worth giving him a tasty dish if only to see the sparkle in his eyes.

Some years ago I went with a party of my Old Comrades for a tour of the Battlefields. We visited Villers sur Simon and the coach pulled up outside a farm. I was the first to alight when I saw an old and decrepit man and when I went over to him he turned out to be our Urinoir. He remembered us and all the games we used to get up to. Needless to say we took him along to the nearest *estaminet*.

The pleasant days at Villers, much to our regret, eventually drew to a close, and we had orders to pack the cooker and limber ready for moving the next day.

The whole of the transport was horse–drawn and as our cooker when laden was very heavy, we had two carthorses called Ginger and Herbie. They were lovable animals and faithfully pulled our cooker for many many miles in France and Belgium, often into very dangerous sections of the line.

12 St. Amand—Halloy—Souastre— Hébuterne

On 6 May we assembled with the Company outside the billet, and waited for the cooker to be drawn out to fall in the rear of the Company. When the cooker rumbled through the gateway there was a huge bunch of lilac tied to the smoking chimney. This was the final act of devotion of poor Urinoir. He was terribly upset at our leaving and the tears ran down his face as we said the last farewells and marched off. We should not have been allowed to have the lilac on the chimney, but Urinoir's grief was so genuine that we had not the heart to take it down, and so waited until we were out of sight before untying the bouquet.

The Battalion halted at Couterelle, and there we issued tea from the cooker by the roadside. We carried on after till we arrived at St. Amand, where we were put into billets. There were batteries of 9.2 howitzers in the village and one of these was close to us. Whenever they fired the shots passed right over the billet, and down would come a shower of tiles from the roof. The Battalion spent about a fortnight there and occupied the time mostly in going up the line on digging fatigues. On several occasions our comrades were out all night, and then we used to stay up to make tea for them on their return in the early hours of the morning.

We left St. Amand on 20 May, and moved to Halloy where on arrival the cookers were drawn into an orchard and, after having served tea and unloaded the limber, we turned into a barn for a sleep at 2am.

The water supply in the village was very poor, and the water carts had to make three trips daily to a spot about three miles away.

The cooker was sent away to Ordnance for repair, so we had to carry on cooking on a trench fire made with iron bars and bricks.

There was plenty of football and Battalion sports were held. After staying at Halloy for twelve days, we pushed on again for another ten miles until we arrived at Souastre. The Battalion was billeted in huts made of corrugated iron and canvas, the roofs of which were camouflaged. We stayed there for the night, and early the next afternoon the Battalion left for the trenches at Hébuterne. The cookers followed later and on the way up we stopped at Bayencourt to pick up the Company's rations at the transport line. Eventually, after dark, we arrived at Hébuterne, a village about four hundred yards behind the front line trenches.

Part of the Battalion was in the trenches just in front of the village, while the remainder was in reserve in the village itself. We cooked meals and fatigue parties carried the dixies to the platoons up in the trenches.

We occasionally had a walk round in the evenings, but this had to be done very warily as the Germans had a nasty habit of suddenly sweeping the village with machine gun fire. One night Macpherson, a fellow cook, was standing on the cooker attending to the dixies when a machine gun bullet ricocheted off the cooker chimney. Much too close for his liking!

On 8 June the Battalion was relieved by the Rangers, and moved to 'The Keep' in the village. This was the end part of the village, in which the roads and byways had been barricaded and strongly defended by machine guns. Our horses arrived and drew our cooker into 'The Keep' so that we could be with the Company. In addition to our equipment we carried with us three– cane bottomed chairs that we had 'scrounged' in the village. We found a billet in a shell-shattered farmhouse, and soon after our arrival a big shell came whizzing over our heads, and a large piece fell in the midden about ten yards away.

The Company spent the time on digging stunts. We spent Whitsun there, and on 13 June moved back again to our old position in the village, and the Battalion occupied the trenches in front.

Profiting by previous experience, we placed the cooker behind a brick wall to avoid being hit by machine gun bullets which had a habit of whistling past us as we were working. The mud was so thick that we obtained three trench boards from the Royal Engineers' dump to place round the cooker. Trench boards were similar to a wooden ladder with slats to allow the water to drain off and so did not get buried in the mud.

The Germans' artillery was very lively, and every now and then they 'strafed' the village. The machine gun fire also made it decidedly unsafe at times to venture out of the billet. One shell hit 'D' Company's billet (called 'The Grand Hotel') and four of them were wounded. One Sunday we received a shock for we were calmly sitting at tea when the Germans put some 5.9 shells over our billet. The first two shells skimmed the roof, and the third landed in the garden behind. We decided to shift and went along to the sergeants' billet where there was a cellar.

The Fusiliers relieved us and the Battalion moved down the line in daylight. The roads were marked by the German artillery so that we had to wait until darkness before we could move down with the cooker. We left Hébuterne, therefore, about 11.15pm and marched to St. Amand. The Battalion had about sixty casualities during this spell at Hébuterne.

We left St. Amand the next day with the Battalion for Pas, where we were billeted in corrugated iron huts.

While we were at Pas, the cooks were served out with khaki drill tunics, and when we appeared arrayed in these the excitement in the Company was intense, for the rumour spread that the Battalion was going to Egypt, but unfortunately they were doomed to disappointment.

One day about a dozen German planes came over to bomb the camp. They missed their objective, however, and dropped their cargo on the village of Pas. One 'Tommy' was killed and two others were wounded. There were also casualties amongst the civilians and our ambulances arrived to pick up the wounded. The invaders were finally driven off by our own planes.

Unfortunately our 'skipper', Captain Anderson, left to go to England. On leaving he made a farewell speech, and was visibly moved. We assembled to see him off, and he rode away to the strains of the pipes playing 'Will ye no come back again'. We were all sorry to lose him for he was a good Officer, and we would have done anything for him. Lt. Brown Constable took over command of 'D' Company.

On 27 June we moved up with the cooker in advance of the Battalion, to Bayencourt. All the inhabitants had left the village under military orders. The place was bristling with guns. The Battalion arrived about an hour and a half after us, and we made tea for the Company. There was a garden at the rear of our billet, in which strawberries, and red and black currants were growing. Needless to say we soon helped ourselves.

The Germans shelled the village with high explosive shells, killing two Rangers and wounding several others.

13 Opening of Battle of The Somme

On 30 June the Battalion left Bayencourt to go into action at Hébuterne.

About 9pm the horses arrived and drew the cooker back to the transport line. This was a place known to the troops as the 'Happy Valley', and lay between Coigneux and Souastre. On our arrival there, we made a 'bivvy' by placing our ground sheets over the pole of the limber, and about midnight we crawled under to sleep. All night long our guns were pounding the German trenches, and we could hear the constant rumble of ammunition columns going up to feed the guns.

The Battalion went 'over the top' on the left of Gommecourt Wood at 7.30am (1 July 1916). Rumours began to circulate, but we could get no definite news. Soon, wounded began to pass us on the way to the village of Coigneux, close by. Reinforcements and ammunition passed us on the way up to the trenches, and about midday German prisoners arrived, and fifty of them were placed in a barbed wire enclosure adjoining a Royal Engineers' dump. Some of the prisoners were wounded, and all presented a very sorry spectacle. Later they were taken farther down the line by a party of cavalry with drawn swords.

At 4.30pm Peachey, a 'B' Company cook, and I went up to Hébuterne to make tea for the Battalion—or rather the survivors. We carried all the necessary tackle as it would have been impossible to get a limber up. The road into the village was being heavily shelled by the Germans, so we decided to go over the plain that lay behind the village. This was bristling with guns and as we were going along we heard a shout, and a battery of '18 pounders' let fly over our heads. We arrived outside the village but the enemy was shelling so severely that it was impossible to enter and parts of the village were on fire. We lay down in the open for an hour or so and, when the shelling somewhat slackened, made our way into the village, where we intended to make the tea in a shattered house.

Water had to be obtained from another shell-stricken house, and this proved to be a ticklish job, for as we were carrying the petrol can to get the water, we suddenly had to throw ourselves flat on th ground, to avoid being hit by a hail of machine gun bullets. We go back all right, and found a big boiler in which we made a fire. W were in the act of pouring the tea into the petrol cans when a 'Whiz Bang' landed about five yards from the door of the room in which w were working and wounded a fellow who was standing outside. Som of the 'Scottish' stragglers were sprawled around us in a state of utte exhaustion. We made all the tea we could, and then put the stopper on the cans and stood them along the wall so that as the troops cam in, they could help themselves. This was all we could do as, of course it was impossible to get the tea up to the trenches.

The Battalion had gone into action 856 strong, but after havin taken four lines of German trenches, had to retire to our own front lin through lack of reinforcements. Casualties were very heavy an amounted to over 600, leaving only about 230 of the Battalion left (We heard later that shortly after we left a shell had landed in th room in which we had made tea, and had scattered all the tins).

There was nothing else we could do, so at 10pm we set off back t the transport line. We picked our way stealthily out of Hébuterne The main road was being heavily shelled, and it would have been fata to have taken that route, so we decided to return across the plain to th rear of the village. At last we arrived at Sailly, where we found 'A' and 'C' Companies' cookers. The Battalion was to be relieved, and wa going back to Sailly. 'B' and 'D' Companies were still at the transport line. As, under the circumstances, four cookers were not necessary ir view of the Battalion's reduced numbers.' Peachey and I carried or therefore, to rejoin our cookers at the transport line. We were jus passing through Bayencourt when one of the Military police came ou of a sentry box, which was barricaded with sandbags, and stopped us. He asked us where we were going and if we had passes. We gave him the necessary information, but as we had no passes we were detained. We were placed in a billet with some fellows of a Lewis Gun team, and a guard was placed over us. We had no coats or groundsheets, and as a result spent a very cold night; furthermore there was no food. Next morning we were all lined up outside the billet, and the Provost Marshal came along. Peachey was explaining what we had been doing, but the PM seemed unconvinced, and as the matter seemed to be getting somewhat awkward I blurted out in desperation 'Well if you don't believe us ask our Quartermaster, who is at our transport line near Coigneux'. He decided to verify our statement. Shortly after, therefore, we set off guarded by a mounted escort complete with swords and lances. The sight of the two of us, marching along the road with mounted men on each side created quite a stir among the passers by. When we arrived at the Transport field we were taken straight to Major Webb, the Quartermaster.

The leader in charge of the escort party said 'These men say that they are two of your cooks', to which Major Webb replied 'That is so'. Then the reply came back 'But they had no passes, Sir'. Major Webb turned to us and said 'Why did you not get passes'. We were so astonished because to our knowledge he had never issued a pass in his life! Major Webb then turned to the escort and said 'That's all right, I'll deal with these men'. Mission accomplished, the escort about turned and went off complete with swords and lances. As soon as they had gone, Major Webb turned on his heels and went back into his store, and never said a word to us then or at any other time.

Major Webb was quite a character and he was tough. The Transport used to go up every night to the trenches to take the rations to the troops and although the Major, even in those days, was getting on in years, he went up every night with them despite the weather, riding his charger 'Lightning'. However that animal got his name I shall never know since I never saw him do more than a gentle amble.

At one time we had a cook-in-charge who must have been psychic, for he always seemed to sense when a cookhouse inspection was in the offing, because when that happened he was invariably missing. On one occasion, the Colonel, the Adjutant, and the Major all descended upon us suddenly. Needless to say our 'psychic' friend was missing as usual and I was left 'holding the baby'. The Colonel thoroughly inspected the cookhouse and then sampled the food. He seemed satisfied, but suddenly shot an awkward question at me. I thought deeply for a moment and then gave a reply. The whole party then left, but Major Webb returned some time later and said to me 'Dolden, as long as you have got as good an excuse next time, that will suit me'. A polite way of calling me a liar!—and he was not far wrong.

The Battalion moved up the line again about 8.30pm to Foncquevillers, a village to the left of Hébuterne. 'B' and 'D' Company cookers followed later. We drew into the village and after having drawn our cooker into a yard, we found a cellar in which there were beds constructed of wood and wire. The Battalion was 'in dugouts in an open field in front of the village. The next day the enemy shelled heavily, and when the firing had ceased the Town Major came along and ordered us to put the cooker under cover, as he thought the smoke from the chimney was the cause of the shelling. One night shelling broke out as the transport arrived with the rations and we had to take refuge in our cellar. Major Webb and Mr Emsley, the Transport Officer, came along too, and the latter was wounded later on his return through the village. The shelling was continued until the early hours of the morning. After four days we were relieved by the Queen Victoria Rifles, and the Battalion moved off about 5pm. We had to wait for darkness, as transport could not move along the road during daylight. When our horses arrived we hooked in and set off down to Souastre where we found a billet in a farm with wire beds. We remained there for three days, during which the Company had baths. We supplied the water from the cooker and a trench fire. The bathing took all day, as the process of heating the water was somewhat slow.

The Brigade assembled in a field outside the village, and the Army Corps commander and the Divisional General thanked the Brigade for the work done on 1 July. We then learned that the objective had been reached, for we had merely been a containing force and not the main attack. The object was to cause a concentration of masses of the enemy and their artillery, and to hold them, in order to relieve the pressure on the troops making the main attack further south on the Somme.

We certainly attracted hordes of the enemy, for the initial attacks farther down on the Somme were carried out with relatively few casualties.

On 10 July, as the Company was so few in numbers due to its recent casualties, I returned to my Platoon Number 13 and so for a time ceased to be a cook. Falling in with the Company at 3.15pm we moved off to relieve the 8th Middlesex Regiment at Hébuterne. Just as we entered the village our guns started a bombardment. On arriving at the trench that we were to occupy, I was detailed with a party under Corporal Anderson to hold a bombing sap. This was a communication trench which had been blocked with sandbags, and in parts the mud came over our hose tops, so that the outlook was far from promising. We got settled down about 7pm and then began to keep watch. Just before dark we all 'Stood to' with fixed bayonets, and from 10 to 11pm I went on guard with another member of the platoon while the others turned in for a rest. When our time was up we awakened the troops and ourselves went off for a sleep. This was no easy matter, for there was no place to lie down, but we found some seats made with sandbags on the parapet and, after putting our waterproof sheets over the top to keep the rain out, endeavoured to snatch some sleep. This was only fitful, however, for our position was far too cramped for comfort.

Next night a sergeant and a party of us were sent out as an advance bombing post in 'No Man's Land'. We climbed over the parapet, and stealthily wended our way some hundred yards in front until we got to a barricade in a shell-battered trench. There we took up our positions with rifle and bombs in hand. German star shells were going up all round. A Brigade was out digging on our right, and after midnight the Germans evidently discovered them, for a terrific fusillade started. First the machine guns rattled out, and then followed the dreaded 'Minenwerfer' (German trench mortars). Our artillery soon got to work, but by degrees the din died down. The extreme quietness after the great din was almost as terrifying, and we felt absolutely alone and stranded out there in the open. There was a 'Scottish' patrol out in front of us, of which we had not been warned. They came upon a party of Germans, and had to retire to the trench with two casualties. We saw them pass us on their way back to the trench and so we were left out there with the knowledge that a German patrol was prowling around. We all felt mighty uncomfortable, but fortunately none of the enemy came our way, and just before dawn, according to orders, we crept back to the trench.

The next morning at breakfast time, the enemy fired on us with trench mortars. The shells dropped far too close to be comfortable, for the earth thrown up as they hit the ground filled our tea mugs. That night we again went out to the advance bombing post.

The next day we were relieved, and went to a trench farther back. This was the original front line, and there we were able to sleep in a dugout. This was a great relief, because for the last three days our position had been so cramped we had not been able to lie down to sleep.

At dawn on 14 July, we could see a bombing raid being carried out on the right by the 4th Royal Gloucesters. It was a very wonderful sight to see the bombs bursting all along the line. But a sight best witnessed from a distance. Shortly after the raid, the British started a bombardment, and smoke was sent over from a trench in front of us. Directly the enemy saw the smoke they immediately opened up with their machine guns, and bullets came rattling against the parapet and whizzing over our heads. They then peppered us with shrapnel and high explosives.

That night I again went to the advance bombing post. We noticed that the Germans were not putting up any star shells on our immediate front line. This seemed suspicious, and looked as though they had a working party out, or possibly patrols. About midnight a 'Scottish' patrol that had been put in front, retired on us suddenly, with the news that they had encountered two German patrols numbering about twenty, and this set us on the alert. Our own patrol retired to the trench behind, and left three of us out there in 'No Man's Land' on our own to hold up any German that might come along. Very soon we spotted the Germans and we grasped our rifles and bombs. We knew that if anything happened we should not stand an earthly chance, for we had orders not to retire under any circumstances, but to attack any patrol that came along, and by so doing would alert the troops in the trench behind. At 2.30am our relief came up, but under the circumstances we could not go back and leave them to it, and so we stopped to give them any necessary help.

Now six in all, we lay and waited. We could hear Germans digging in front. Fortunately the mauraders kept off and eventually we crept back to the trench. There we found that the Lewis gunners had to stand ready as well, as trouble had been expected.

During the night a 'Scottish' patrol brought in a private of the Fusiliers who had been lying out in an unoccupied trench in 'No Man's Land' since 1 July—in all thirteen days. He had been unconsious for most of the time, and only remembered two dawns. Despite the long exposure great hopes were entertained for his recovery. He did, in fact, fully recover and on one noted occasion he was able to attend as a visitor a 1st Battalion reunion at the headquarters of the London Scottish Regiment in Bùckingham Gate. He was, in fact, a guest of one of the members of the patrol that found him.

On the night of 16 July, during my spell of duty at the advanced post 'C' Company, with 'D' Company's Lewis gunners, carried out a raid on the enemy's trenches in front. A line of figures left the trench;

each man had his hands, face and knees blackened, and the brightness of all bayonets had been dimmed. Silently the line disappeared beyond our own barbed wire. Very soon after the excitement began, for our fellows were spotted when they were about seventy yards from the German trench, and the machine guns opened out on them. The bullets began to whistle round our post to such an extent that it was impossible for us to remain lying in the open, and we had to make a dart for a communication trench close by, called 'New Welcome Street'. Mr Warlock of 'A' Company sent up a red rocket as a signal to our own artillery to open fire, as it was impossible for our chaps to get through the enemy wire. Our guns got going soon after, and so did the Germans' unfortunately for us. Soon their shells and trench mortar bombs were bursting round our trench. I was sent to the trench behind with a message, and on my return I had to go through thick oozy mud which came nearly up to my waist.

The raiding party at last received orders to retire. They sustained only two casualties which, considering the heavy fire, was truly remarkable. Later on, our bombing party received orders to retire also. When at last I was able to get to a dugout, I turned my attention to my feet. My boots were filled with mud and water, and my hose tops and socks were soaking. I put on a new pair of socks, and so was a little more comfortable. During the excitement of the previous night the rain had fallen incessantly, and consequently my overcoat, kilt and ground sheet were soaked. I found a couple of sandbags, and Lamont spread his overcoat over the two of us and so I got a little sleep. On 17 July we were relieved after eight nerve–wracking days. We marched back to Bayencourt and by the time we arrived were very nearly 'done', and I went along and billeted with the cooks.

There were shower baths at Sailly which we found consisted of three miserable squirts of water, and nearly cold water at that. It would have been more appropriate if they had been called 'April Showers'.

I was put on unloading timber to reinforce the roof of a dugout for the Divisional Staff at Sailly. We first had to load huge tree trunks on to a GS (General Service) wagon. It took about twenty of us to lift one log, and the wagon then took the load for a distance of about a quarter of a mile to the dugout, where we had to unload it. This proved to be a dangerous business, and one fellow narrowly missed getting his leg broken by a falling log, but luckily we just turned the timber in time. I very nearly got crushed myself by another falling log.

On one occasion we went to Hébuterne to dig gun emplacements for a 9.2 Howitzer battery of the RGA. We felt pretty sore with the artillery at this, and felt that they should do their own dirty work. After six days at Bayencourt we moved up again to the trenches at Hébuterne, and I again found myself in the old bombing position in 'Whiskey Street'. We took up our abode in an ammunition dugout, and I slept on a dump of Mills bombs. I should certainly have been well in for a lift if anything had set the bombs off.

At dark we went out again to the advance post in 'No Man's Land'. There was a pioneer battalion (The Cheshires) digging in the trench, so we had to go nearer to the German lines to act as a covering party while the digging was in progress. The next night we had just been relieved from the bombing post about midnight, when a Captain of the REs. wanted us to guide him to the advance post. We did this, and it then transpired that he wanted us to act as a covering party to his men while they were working out there. There was no need for a covering party, but the real trouble was that the Officer had 'the wind up' badly. He fairly gave us the 'pip', for as we walked on in front he and his party would crouch down every time a German star shell went up. In an endeavour, therefore, to create confidence in his party, we strutted about 'No Man's Land' as if we did not know what fear was. Little did he know our real feeling. The party carried out their task staking out a new trench, whilst we kept our weather eye open. When the work was finished we all returned to the trench about 3am.

On 27 July we were relieved by 'C' Company and 'D' Company then went back to 'Cross Street'. This was a series of dugouts in an orchard just in front of Hébuterne. Each dugout was about ten feet below the ground, and held from fifteen to twenty persons. The dugouts were necessary, as there were guns in the orchard and consequently the place came in for a good deal of shelling from the enemy.

After dark we were sent up again to deepen the old British front line. The work went off fairly quietly, for there was only a sniper and an occasional machine gun to worry us.

Drafts had arrived from time to time, and the Battalion was fairly strong again, so that the Company Sergeant Major sent for me and told me I was to go back to the cooker. I got my things together and went back to the village where I found the cooker in a yard and the cooks billeted in a cellar. The next morning I was at the old trade again.

When the meat arrived next day its presence was so very obvious that we had suspicions as to its goodness. We accordingly got the MO to have a look at it. He immediately condemned part of it, and the remainder we had to wash in permanganate of potash.

On 31 July the Battalion left the trenches and moved down to Sailly au Bois. We waited for the horses to come up after dark and pulled out of the village, arriving at Sailly about midnight. The Battalion stayed there for four days, during which there was a kit inspection for the cooks. By dint of borrowing the articles we lacked we managed to present a full kit. The borrowed articles were duly returned after the inspection!

On 4 August, the Battalion moved up to Hébuterne, again to relieve the Royal Fusiliers in the trenches. We went up later after dark with the cooker. On the Bank Holiday our artillery strafed the Germans furiously, but fortunately for us there was no return fire. Our artillery again got busy; this time, however, there was a reply from the Germans just as the rations arrived. One of the shells burst in the yard outside our billet and there was a stampede to the cellar. Later on the German artillery gave us another warm time. In the morning they shelled the farther end of the village. About midday, however, they started again—nearer and nearer the shells came, till with a terrific shriek one came over the billet, knocking a wall down just opposite. This last was too much of a good thing, so we took to our cellar, and very hurriedly too.

About 11pm we moved down to Bayencourt and, as we passed, the guns on the plain at the back of the village were blazing away. We stayed at Bayencourt for five days, during which time there was a full parade of the Brigade just outside the village, when the Divisional General presented the medals won in the 1 July Battle.

On the night of 11 August one of the cooks went up in advance with the Battalion to Hébuterne, while the rest of us followed next day with the cooker. We arrived at about 11pm at our old billet. We found to our cost that the Germans were not going to leave us alone for they let fly at us and we had to make a dive for the cellar. We only stayed three days in Hébuterne this trip, but on each day we had to scuttle for our lives, away from the German shelling. They were evidently in a nasty mood as a result of the recent action. In addition, a German plane came over and dropped bombs on us. We saw quite a lot of the inside of our cellar that trip. Luckily there was no direct hit on the cellar, otherwise it would have been a sorry day for us because the roof was none too strong.

On 19 August 'A' and 'D' Company's cookers had orders to go down to Bayencourt, so we packed up and waited for the transport. The shelling on the road was fairly heavy, and Corporal Gunn who was in charge of the transport was shot through the heart and died instantly. Our horses arrived and hooked in, and while we were waiting for the transport column to start back, the machine gun bullets were striking the roadway. We left sometime after midnight, and on arriving at Bayencourt we pulled in at our old billet. We found this in the occupation of the Kensingtons, so we could not take over our old shed. We left the cooker in the yard, therefore, and at 2.30am in the morning went in search of a place to sleep. Macpherson, one of the cooks, led the way, holding a lighted candle. We went to see if the old canteen was empty, with the object of sleeping there. The old lady of the house heard us and got into a violent rage, and properly went off the 'deep end' at us, shouting that we were thieves and robbers and a whole lot of very uncomplimentary French remarks. She seemed to think we were after the vegetables. The idea! We slunk off, and at last found an empty room where we dumped our things and before very long were fast asleep.

The next morning we moved the cooker to a suitable position, and were ready for the Company on their arrival from Hébuterne about 5pm.

In the evening one of our captive balloons broke loose, and was carried towards the German lines. When just over our heads, one of the occupants descended in a parachute. The balloon drifted further and a second man descended. This time, unfortunately, the parachute failed to open and the poor fellow fell with a rush and was smashed to a pulp just outside Sailly. Our own anti–aircraft guns fired on the balloon and at the third shot hit it. The balloon burst into flames and fell slowly to the ground. We heard later that the poor fellow who was killed was Basil Hallam, the music hall artist well known for his singing of the song 'Gilbert the Filbert'.

Pages of the author's diary with notes of the attack on the Hollenzollern Redoubt at Hulluch during the Battle of Loos, 13th October, 1915 (pages 44 and 45).

(Right)
Some survivors of the 1st
Battalion London Scottish
Regiment after the Battle of
Messines 31st October, 1914
– Hallowe'en! The Regiment
was the first Territorial unit
to go into action in World
War I. (Courtesy Imperial
War Museum).

(Below)
The author's Regiment in a
typical shell-torn front line
area during the early stages
of the War. (Courtesy
Imperial War Museum).

The War's devastation of Vermelles village(page 20).

The ruins of the church at Hébuterne lie as a shelled heap of rubble on top of what was once its cemetary.

The author at the time of his enlistment in
the London Scottish Regiment, 1914.

The author holding a section of the 'Lone
Tree' (page 30), with its embedded bullet,
during a visit to the original site many
years later.

Winter dress on the Western Front; sheepskin jackets (left) and leather jerkin (right)

S ILLY

Horse-drawn World War I field kitchens with cookers in action (above) *and on the move* (below). (*Courtesy Imperial War Museum*).

The destruction of much of Arras by shell damage (right *and* below) *is all too apparent in these contemporary photographs.*

The London Scottish parade out of Charing Cross station, London on their return from Germany as part of the Army of Occupation, following the Armistice.

14 The Somme

Our Quartermaster had a habit of which we hardly approved. He would boast to the other Quartermasters in the Brigade that his cooks got closer to the enemy than theirs. That this was no idle boast will become apparent from time to time in these pages.

On 21 August the 17th Division took over our position in the 4th Army Corps, and so we left the Hébuterne sector. The Battalion marched by Companies down to Halloy, arriving some time about 4pm, and were billeted in canvas huts of the good old army non–waterproof type. We moved off again next day to Doullens, where we entrained in cattle trucks, forty men to a truck. About 9pm we detrained at St. Riquier, and then followed a march of six miles to the little village of Drucat. The Company was put into billets, but we found that, as usual, the cooks had been forgotten, and so after letting forth a flow of real Army oaths we set out to find one for ourselves. We got settled at last and then, after having had something to eat, sat down to wait for the cooker which had gone with the transport by road. In the early hours of the morning we were awakened to find that the cooker had just arrived. We found it left by the roadside, the horses having gone off to the transport field. We unpacked the limber and got ready for breakfast. We presented a queer spectacle with the dixies and tackle on the roadside, and would have looked very appropiate on the title page of the song 'Where my Caravan is Rested! We stayed at Drucat for twelve days, during which time the cooker was sent away for repairs, and we had to cook on a trench fire.

I was inoculated again, and was very sore and stiff for a couple of days.

On 2 September 1916, we got to bed at 11.45pm, but were up again at *12.30am* in time to have everything packed and ready when the Battalion moved off. The dixies filled with meat and vegetables were handed to the Platoon to carry, and they were far from keen on the job, and at 3.45am we left Drucat. In the darkness the sound of dixie lids falling off could be heard, accompanied by a good deal of cursing from those who were carrying them. The route, though short, was very bad for we were very much delayed by the thick mud in some of the byways. Just before daybreak we arrived at St. Riquier, by which time it was quite noticeable that those who had been carrying dixies were in a snappy mood. At the station we were put into carriages, five a side. This on the face of it does not sound so bad, but when five–a–side sets of packs and equipment were included we could just get in, but only just, and where one's limbs first rested there they had to remain for the entire journey. We passed several prisoner of war camps, and could also see Germans working along the banks of the river Somme. We passed through Amiens and stopped at Corbie, where we detrained and set off for Daours. We had almost arrived when one of the Divisional Staff rode up in a motor car and informed our Colonel that our destination had been altered at the last moment, and we had to 'about turn' and march right back to Corbie, and from there we set off to Sailly le Sec where we arrived about 3.30pm. No billets for the cooks had been found yet again, so we 'scrounged' around for one which we found just as the cooker arrived. When we had finished work for the day we got the old lady of the house adjoining our billet to fry us some eggs. She was a cheery old soul, and made us very comfortable. Later we turned into bed in a loft and went to sleep in some straw that we had found. Below us, and fast asleep in his sty lay our immediate neighbour, a big fat pig. Although we could not see him, his presence was impressed upon us by the strong aroma wafting up from his sty. A little black dog appeared from nowhere and attached himself to us.

The Battalion was put under orders to be ready to move at half an hour's notice, and we had to bustle about, therefore, to get everything packed and be ready to move at short notice. When we were about half–packed the transport sergeant dashed up to say that the Brigade transport had left. We had to dump a lot of stuff and threw the cover over the limber and rope up straightaway. We set off, and it took us about a quarter of an hour to catch up with the Brigade transport. A wearying march followed, for the whole Division tramped across tracks temporarily laid across ploughed fields. At one spot the cooker became firmly embedded in the mud. The whole transport had to charge over the top of a steep incline, and our cooker horses failed to rise to the occasion. At last, with a great struggle and with an extra horse, we got over the hillock and were on our way again.

After tramping through thick mud for four solid hours, we at last arrived at our destination—a camp situated in a howling wilderness about one and a half miles north of Bray. There the cookers were drawn up in line in front of the camp.

We were now in the back area of the Somme, and the Division was standing by, as a reserve to the troops carrying on the Somme battle.

Water was again the trouble, and we had to wait for water tanks to be brought up on motor lorries. Our GS wagons arrived about sixteen hours late, as they had got stuck in the mud. We got on with the dinner as well as we could, for we had to stand packed ready for moving at half an hour's notice.

We were helping to get a passing wagon out of the mud when the alarm was given. The Battalion was issued with bombs, and set off before us. The rain came pelting down as we started off with the transport. All over the vast plain there were camps, transport and troops. The whole area was covered with thick oozy mud, and wagons and limbers were struggling along. We got a little way when we came to a halt, and after a wait the cookers were turned round and taken to the transport line again. In the evening we had to make up tea and sugar rations in sandbags, and these were taken up to the Battalion by the ration limbers.

The next morning one of our captive balloons ascended just in front of us, and very soon after a German shell burst and the balloon came toppling down. A little later the Germans shelled neighbouring transport lines and the horses stampeded, but no damage was done. We were lying near Mametz Wood and Fricourt, where there had recently been heavy fighting, and some of my friends and I strolled over to have a look round. Passing over the old British front line, we kept on over what had once been 'No Man's Land'. This was pitted with tremendous shell holes and the earth was torn up in all directions.

Just before getting to the old German front lines we came across five or six mine craters. Evidently the Germans had tried to stop the British advance by springing mines. The craters varied from thirty to fifty feet across. The German line behind was literally blown to smithereens and it was difficult to distinguish in places what were holes and what were trenches. Pools of blood—red water were lying about, and by one such pool there was a small wooden cross erected with the inscription 'The Body of an unknown British Soldier lies here'. Nothing but the mound and the water, stained probably by his own blood, to mark that poor fellow's last resting place.

German bombs were lying about in all directions, and there were numerous 'dud' shells which, of course, had to be carefully avoided. We entered a German trench and explored one of the dugouts, and endeavoured to find the bottom. We went down thirty five steps and came upon a gallery where we found a store of ammonal saltpetre in small packets. We went down another flight of seventy five steps. The air was getting very foul and heavy and, as we had no candle, we had to give it up and return to the top. We came to the conclusion that as there were over a hundred and ten steps we must have found a mine shaft. On our way back we passed lights flashing signals to the artillery in the distance.

The guns were rumbling in one incessant roar firing on the retiring enemy in front. All the plain was twinkling with myriads of light from the little shelters.

The Battalion, after leaving, had gone into action and had repulsed two German counter attacks. About 8pm we received orders to move up the line with the cooker, as the Battalion was being relieved from the front line and was going into the reserve trenches in the rear. For two hours we struggled along on an atrocious road. Our driver found every shell hole I think there was to be found, and the cooker very nearly came to grief three or four times. The guns were blazing away by the roadside, and in all directions British 'Caterpillars' passed taking heavy guns up the line into action. French transport and ambulances passed us on their way down. Troops were everywhere. We got to the Brigade dump about two miles beyond Maricourt, and there waited in a valley near a trench called 'Chimpanzee Trench'. Evidently we were not expected, for there was a long wait before we were able to get into position. All the while there was a furious British bombardment in progress. A line of French 75in guns were lined up on the ridge just above our heads, and we got the full benefit of the Germans' return shelling when they tried to put the French guns out of action. We had to leave the cookers in the open and take refuge in a trench nearby. We made tea for the Battalion about 1am and then each of us found a little 'funk-hole' to sleep in. These were shallow holes scooped out of the side of the trench.

On getting up next morning we found that there was no water in the cooker so we pooled the water from all four cookers and were thus able to serve up a short ration of tea to the Company, After this there

84

was no water left, for the water carts were empty too.

About 10am the Germans gave us a very warm time, for they shelled our valley all over. A gun pit was blown in, and an ammunition limber was also caught. One half of it went up in the air, and horses were cut loose in all directions. On the brow of the hill at the back of us an old Boer War type of ambulance was standing. A shell landed near it; the horses threw up their heads, but stood still. The next shell fell square on the ambulance. When the smoke cleared nothing was left of the ambulance, horses or wounded, and all that could be seen was the centre pole lying on the road. Things quietened down after a bit, and we were able to move about again. Shelling started up again later, and one of the gun posts near us was threatened with destruction. The horses came dashing up to draw out the guns and they hooked in and had just left the pit when a shell landed in the middle of them. By a miracle no one was hurt, and the big guns with eight horses on each went helter skelter up the hill and over the ridge into comparative safety. The next day our guns carried on the bombardment. After a time we grew accustomed to the noise, but by degrees the continual shrieking and whining of the shells got on one's nerves, and one felt a terrible yearning for quietness again.

On 9 September our horses arrived and drew the cooker back to the transport line. The walk back in the blazing sun was very trying. While resting on the way the horses of one of the wagons bolted and very nearly ran over us; the driver was flung from his seat and the wheels missed his head by inches. The horses, however, were eventually stopped. The Battalion went into action at 5.30pm and sustained 271 casualties, seventy of which were in 'D' company.

The next day the Battalion came down to a field about two miles in front of us, and so we met them on their way down. We made tea for them, and then they carried on, and when the last party had gone we packed up and followed. We lost our way, but at last found the Battalion at about 5.30am sleeping in an open field. We simply crept under the cooker, therefore, with our overcoats over us, and snatched a few hours sleep.

On 12 September I saw tanks for the first time, for two of them crawled slowly past us on their way up. Two days later a Naval 12in gun was brought up on a railway that had been built to follow the advance. When the gun was fired the concussion could be felt all over the valley. We left about 9pm the same day and followed the

Battalion, but instead of taking the usual road we travelled by a track set apart for the 1st Cavalry Division. We got to the old Brigade dump at 'Chimpanzee Trench' about midnight when we turned into 'cubby holes' for the night. The Battalion went on in advance to Angle Wood.

There was a tremendous bombardment early next morning. On getting up we found one of the 'Land Crabs' (Tanks) lying in the valley; it had had some slight mishap and was waiting repairs. Later on, another crippled tank came limping out of action.

While at this spot I took the opportunity of exploring Trones Wood. The place was knocked to bits and in the centre there was a German cemetery.

At 9.30pm we were turned out of our 'cubby holes' and had to pack up. When the horses arrived at 2.30am next morning we moved with the cooker farther up the line. It had rained slightly, and consequently our progress was very slow, since the mud was so thick that it took four horses to pull our cooker along. Up and down, and in and out of shell holes we stumbled along on our way to Angle Wood, the resting place of the Battalion. A shell or two exploded near us and helped to quicken our footsteps. We passed numbers of dead horses, and the stench from these fairly took one's breath away. We arrived at our destination at about 5am and took up our positions in a valley known as 'Death Valley'. It was not worth turning in for a sleep, so we remained up to make breakfast for the Company.

During the time we remained in 'Death Valley' we were considerably troubled by hundreds of bluebottles; they were full bodied ones too, and appeared quite bloated. I found out the reason later for their number and rotundity, and the discovery filled me with a feeling of revulsion. I went up on to a ridge above the cooker on a journey of exploration, and at one spot as I put my foot down there was a loud buzzing, and dozens of bluebottles flew up. There to my astonishment I saw a face—the face of a dead German. The whole ridge was covered with German and French dead, upon which swarms of bluebottles had settled. These same insects no doubt were going to follow their fellows down into the valley and were going to settle on our food.

We moved down that night to 'Chimpanzee Trench' and there a draft of fifty fellows from the 9th Highland Light Infantry joined us. This was the first occasion on which we had other troops from another

86

regiment drafted to us. The next day the Battalion asked for another cooker to be sent to them at Angle Wood, and so our horses were hooked in and we set off up the line. It rained heavily, and we plodded on laboriously through the thick mud, and by the time we got to Angle Wood and had taken up our old position in 'Death Valley', we were thoroughly soaked through. We found the Battalion looking the picture of misery. Another cook and I started to erect a shelter with our ground sheets, but the heavy rain soon flooded us out. Wet to the skin we served up tea to the Company, and then there was nothing to do but to stand and shiver. The prospect for the night looked black, as everywhere the mud was deep, and in most cases came over one's ankles. There was not the slightest cover anywhere. The rain gave over a little, so I made myself a shelter by covering a shell hole with my ground sheet. A big fire had been lit in another shell hole close by, and a ring of troops was sitting around it, so I went along and joined the group in an attempt to snatch a little comfort. The rain then began to fall again, so I went back to my shelter, where I found that a little dog had settled in my absence. I had not the faintest idea where he had come from, but he was shivering so much and looked so wretched, that I let him stay and we both curled up together. The rain pelted down during the night and I was bitterly cold. Very soon I was lying in a pool and my boots filled with water. The little dog shivered and crept closer to me. A little way off I could see our cooker standing in a veritable sea of mud in the valley, with a group of troops huddled round its fire. Some were even sitting on top with their feet where the dixies usually stood.

Later on the Battalion moved up to the front line. There was another night of utter misery followed by a hopeless dawn, for on going to the cooker I found that during the night someone had tethered a couple of horses to our limber. They had pulled off the whole load, and it was stuck fast in the mud; but worse than that, the horses had scoffed the whole of our bread and biscuit rations, and so we had nothing to eat for the whole day.

We made tea for the part of the Battalion that remained in the valley, about one hundred in all, and soon after the sun broke through the clouds; we hailed the bright beam with as much fervour as if we had been sun worshippers. We welcomed with almost childish delight anything that would add a little brightness to our otherwise dismal surroundings. Our joy, however, was short lived for very soon the rain came streaming down again. Every time a wagon passed us a shower of mud would be flung up, and we would be plastered from head to foot. In addition to our battle with the elements, we had to contend with German shelling. On one occasion we had a particularly warm time, for they 'strafed' the valley with shrapnel and heavy shells. One landed quite close to our cooker, and we had to dart to a trench nearby and remain there for many hours, as it was unhealthy to venture out. At intervals we did come out, but only to be speedily driven back.

Several 'tear gas' shells burst near us making our eyes water and smart badly. Several of the troops were wounded, and one of our ammunition dumps was blown up. All through the shelling the rain fell unceasingly. All day long the wounded were being brought down from the firing line and passed us on stretchers; some were absolutely prostrate with exhaustion and cold, and were being helped along by others. Wagons and limbers which ordinarily only required two horses to pull them, now required six, and in some cases eight, horses to drag them through the mud. Walking even became a matter of extreme difficulty, for the mud clung to one's boots and some men actually lost their boots in the mud. The strain was awful, and we yearned for relief.

The Battalion was later relieved by the Kensingtons, and then took up a position on the top of the ridge just above our cooker in 'Death Valley'.

When darkness fell all lights and fires had to be extinguished, as enemy aircraft were about. On the following day the weather brightened somewhat. The British and French artillery 'strafed' the Germans, and later we got the benefit of the enemy's return fire, for soon their shells were bursting over us.

At 1.30pm we received orders to move down the line. Instead of the usual two horses we had to have six horses to drag our cooker along, and even then they could only just move. We stopped at 'Chimpanzee Trench', where we found 'B' Company's cooker' thinking that was our destination. We only stayed for about half an hour, but it was an exceedingly warm half hour, for the Germans shelled us with heavy shells the whole time. I was standing on the top of the trench watching the bursting of the shells when there was a terrific whizz and I saw a flash of fire about five yards away, and a rush of wind threw me head first into the six foot trench. Everything went black, my ears were throbbing, and my heart momentarily stoppped beating. The smoke and acrid smell from the shell cleared away, and I got up out of the trench. Many were wounded by that shell, and there was a horse standing on the parapet of the trench with half of its face blown away. Despite this terrible wound the animal was standing quite still, except for a twitching of its head. The only merciful thing to do was to destroy the animal, and it was accordingly led away and shot.

We found out later that we should have gone to a trench known as 'Casement' about a mile further down the line, so we got on the road again. When we arrived at 'Casement Trench' we found a 12 inch howitzer gun near. The Germans were shelling the gun, and tried to put it out of action, and of course we came in for the shots. We took over a little corrugated iron shed from the cooks of the 3rd London Fusiliers, and so had some protection from the rain at least. The Battalion was not expected to arrive until after dark, so we made a fire and sat up to make tea for them. I was able to take my boots off for the first time in ten days, and to my surprise my feet were perfectly white and ribbed, but soon recovered after a night's rest.

After a two days' rest the Battalion moved up again to the trenches. Two cookers were sent down to the 'Citadel' and our cooker together with 'B' Company's, went up to 'Chimpanzee Trench'. Here we waited to make tea for the Battalion when they came out of action.

The next day the Battalion went into action near Leuze and Boileau Woods. We made tea for some of the wounded 'Scottish' as they passed us on the way down. Soon after, German prisoners began to arrive, some of whom were in a pitiable condition and must have suffered terribly from our furious shell fire. All day troops were being carried up on a railway track recently laid to keep pace with the advance.

There were no signs of our fellows coming back that night, so we turned in to snatch some sleep. Early the next afternoon we moved up with the cooker to Angle Wood. Wounded Germans, found in Combles after it had been evacuated, were brought past us. The Battalion arrived at 11.30pm and we made tea for them.

The French '75' Batteries were going strong all the morning, and in the evening a party of French 'poilus' arrived, and formally took over 'Angle Wood' from the Battalion. At about 8pm the Battalion was relieved and moved further down the line. We had to wait for our horses, and about six hours after got on the way ourselves. We stumbled on through the black night, and at last arrived at 'Casement Trench'. We had some difficulty in finding the Battalion, but eventually ran them to earth at about 4.30am. We were by that time so fagged out that we simply unlimbered, and crawled under the cooker to sleep. In the early afternoon, the Battalion set off further down, with our cooker following on behind. The distance we marched was ten miles, but the sun was very strong, and made the 'going' extremely difficult, especially as our feet were in a very bad and sore condition. When we arrived at the 'Citadel' we passed a field strewn with dead horses, the result of a German bombing raid the previous night. About 6.30pm we arrived at the village of Ville sur Corbie, where we were billeted with the Company in a barn. For a month we had not seen a house, or any sign of civilisation—nothing but mud and devastation everywhere. When I turned in to sleep that night I took off my clothes for the first time in twenty five days.

We stayed at Ville sur Corbie for two days when, to everyone's disappointment, the Battalion had to go up again into the 'Hell Area'. They moved up at 10am. It was 'D' Company's turn to remain at the transport line, so 'A' and 'B' Company's cookers went up with the Battalion, while 'C' and ourselves remained behind. At 11.30am, therefore, we set off to the 'Citadel' and pulled up at the horse lines. We had about two miles to go for water, and after we had done this we built a little shelter, as we were again in the open. I had just 'turned in' after dark, when I heard the ominous purr of an engine. This was soon followed by explosions, and bombs began to fall round us. This was very disturbing, for we only had a sheet of thin corrugated iron over our heads.

One morning there was wild excitement amongst the troops, for the rumour was circulating that there were ladies around. I turned out with the others to see and, sure enough, striding along the road there were four English nurses. These were the first members of the opposite sex we had seen for a month, and everyone stopped work to behold the fair 'visions'.

The horses used to be taken to a central watering place some distance off. Troughs were arranged in a huge square, and the horses were driven in through a narrow opening. On one occasion I asked our driver to let me take the cooker horses to water. He was only too glad to let someone else do the job for him. The cooker had two heavy draught horses, Herbie and Ginger, and so I set off without a saddle, practically doing the splits on one and leading the other. Everything went off quietly until we got to the watering troughs, but the Cavalry had arrived and there were hundreds of horses at the troughs, and they were all excited to get a drink. My two nags pricked up their ears and made an unexpected dash into the crowd. I was absolutely helpless, for I was hemmed in with horses pushing me in all directions, so I hung on like grim death. However when the horses had slaked their thirst, they sorted themeselves out again, and eventually I got back to our own transport line, where with a feeling of genuine relief I slid from my charger's back.

The Battalion went into action again on 7 October and two days afterwards came down to the 'Citadel'. The next morning we turned out early and, after having served breakfast, set off, together with 'C' Company cooker in advance of the Company. Marching through Fricourt and Mealte, we halted at Ville sur Corbie, and waited there until the Battalion marched to Mericourt, where there were about a hundred motor buses. We clambered into these and soon the whole column was set in motion. We were all filled with unbounding joy when we realised that at last our backs had been turned on the Somme, and all its horrors and miseries. The one outstanding feature of the Somme was the mud. Living with it around one day and night seemed to tap one's vitality. We had already experienced severe shelling, trenches and all the incidences of warfare on other sectors of the line, and so it became merely a question of degree, but after our trip to the Somme I realised what a truly demoralising affect mere mud could have.

One day when I was feeling utterly miserable due to the appalling conditions on the Somme, I received a letter offering me a commission on General Thornton's staff. He was the General in overall command of railway communications with Headquarters in Paris.

It need hardly be said that under the conditions prevailing at the time, the offer was very tempting and I gave a great deal of thought as to whether I should accept it or not. I came to the conclusion, however, that to transfer from the Somme to a post possibly in Paris would require great strength of character if one was not to be undermined morally. After weighing up the pros and cons, therefore, I decided to refuse the commission.

This decision I have never regretted since it enabled me to remain

91

with my comrades with whom I had served for so long, until the end of the War. Furthermore, it afforded me the friendship of those of my old comrades who survived the War, and which has continued ever since, although the passage of time has considerably reduced our numbers.

15 The Armentières Sector

Our fleet of buses rattled through Amiens and at last pulled up outside the little village called St. Vaast en Charissère, just as darkness fell. We left the buses, and two hours later marched off to the village of Fremont, where we were put into billets in which there were wire beds.

We stayed at Fremont for ten days, during which we spent a fairly quiet time. Leave was granted by rotation into the town of Amiens and one Sunday Macpherson and I availed ourselves of the opportunity and made a trip into the town. We spruced ourselves up, a lengthy process for a cook, and paraded at the Orderly room for our passes. Armed with these we set off from Fremont by a short cut over tracks, arriving in Amiens in about an hour and a half. Our first thought was to get a feed, and so we looked round for an inviting looking estaminet. We found one, and straightaway entered and once more sat down at a table with a white tablecloth. We waited a long time and eventually a waitress arrived to whom we gave our order. After some time an omelette arrived, the size of which fell sadly short of our eager expectations, and we demolished it easily in two mouthfuls. We next ordered beefsteak and potatoes, although the fact that we noticed its arrival was a wonder since its size, to say the least, was diminutive, and was about three inches square. The 'feed', though small, was compensated by the bill which was large, and we came away with that 'sinking feeling'. Our appetite was by no means appeased, so we looked round for another estaminet. We struck a good place at last, but as soon as we entered we found it was closing time, and so decided to give dinner a miss, and to wait for tea. In the meantime we paid the Cathedral a visit. Most of the interesting parts were not on view, for all the best mural paintings and statues were protected by barricades of sandbags against damage by air raids. After a look round we found a small patisserie, and we regaled ourselves with coffee and pastries, and received another shock when we got the bill.

We started back at 5.30pm and had a very weary tramp as we lost our way. There was no moon and the night was as black as pitch.

Floundering about over ploughed fields amongst cabbages etc., we came across two other Scottish fellows, one of whom had a compass, and with it tried to guide us home. But we were worse off than ever and as we were walking into the pitch darkness the fellow in front of me suddenly disappeared altogether; very shortly after I fell down a steep embankment about thirty feet deep. At the bottom of this we came across a lonely village. There, someone put us on the right route, but as we were wet through we first went into an estaminet for hot coffee. After a rest we set off to cover the remaining five kilometres to Fremont.

On 20 October we were up at 4 am to get packed ready for moving. It was extremely dark, so that we had to rush round with a flash lamp. It was a very cold but beautiful day as we set off. About 6pm we arrived at our destination. The Battalion, with the exception of 'D' Company, was billeted at Hocquincourt. There were not enough billets for the whole Battalion, so 'D' Company were left at Hallincourt about threequarters of a mile away.

Evening came, and still no billets for the cooks, so we decided to find one for ourselves. We came across an old Frenchman, and asked if he could find us a room for the night. He led us to a farm, and there disclosed to our view a comfortable room with—Ye Gods!—a bed. He apologised profusely because he could not supply us all with beds, but he made a comfortable place on the floor with a bolster, and absolutely refused to accept a single sou for the accommodation. After we had prepared the cooker for the morning we returned to our 'haven of rest'. The old folks came to see us, and with them sundry relations. Before turning in, we cooks tossed for the bed. My luck was in and I won. It was an old four poster and I had not slept between sheets for at least ten months—it felt like heaven. Of course the inevitable fly settled in the ointment, for having found the most comfortable of billets the Company must needs move on, as they were outside the billeting area, and this we did next morning. Before we left, the dear old folks made coffee for us, and fussed round us like hens round their chickens.

We moved into Hocquincourt and waited there till the authorities decided how we were to be disposed of. At last, the colossal mind of the 'Brass Hats' (Staff Officers) came to a decision, and we marched off to another village about two kilometres further on. It boasted of about three farms, and was perched up on a hill, in a small clump of trees. A

94

more desolate place I have rarely seen; it rejoiced under the name of Etalemenite. The cooker was drawn up on the village green, a plot of grass about fifteen feet square. Thank goodness we only stayed there for two days for on the 23 October we went to Hocquincourt. Kerr and Macpherson then left with the cooker in advance, to entrain at Longpré, while Sanders and I followed with the Battalion. We detrained at Merville, and after the transport had been unloaded, we set off to Estaires, about five miles away. After we had made tea for the Company we prepared to turn in for the night. The Battalion was housed in a disused brewery and, of course, 'D' Company was on the top floor, four stories up, so that it was quite a route march to go to bed. When daylight came, and we returned to the cookers, we discovered the reason for the overpowering smell that had assailed us when we had drawn up the cookers on the previous night. Opposite us we found a big building full of hides from recently killed sheep and bullocks, and the floor was swamped with blood.

After some persuasion the church authorities allowed us to sleep in the coal bunkers of the church's heating chamber. It was decidedly dirty, but nevertheless warm.

On 27 October we moved up to Laventie, a village about two miles behind the trenches, and there were billeted in some old racing stables. The next day the Battalion moved into the trenches. Owing to the nature of the country, relief could be carried out in daylight. The cooker was left behind in Laventie and one cook remained with it while the other cooks separated and each went with a platoon into the line. Our camp dixies etc., were carried by the Platoon. At 10am we set off in small parties in order to minimize casualties from shell fire. As we approached the trenches we walked in single file. 'D' Company was in reserve and occupied three posts, the 'Hougemont Post' on the right, 'Dead End Post' in the centre and 'Picantin Post' on the left. As Number 13 Platoon occupied 'Picantin Post' I went along with them. The platoon was put into two wooden huts, and close by there was a little wooden cookhouse, over which I reigned supreme. The water arrangements were quite good, for there was a pump near. In fact, we found out that there was precious little else but water in the sector, and our post was amongst hedges and swamps some thousand yards behind the front line trench.

After having lit a fire, I went round to the other posts to see how the other cooks were getting on. When I returned I made tea for the boys, and then retired to my billet for the night. A big bombardment started up towards dark, and the air was rent with the bursting of German trench mortar shells. After I had turned in the Platoon were called out as a German attack was expected; this did not materialise however, and they returned at about four in the morning.

We stayed in the post for four days, during which time I made breakfast, dinner and tea for the boys in my little cookhouse. We spent Hallowe'en there and, as far as our limited resources would allow, celebrated by a dinner, the principal dish of which was the somewhat undignified, though under the circumstances not to be despised, sausages and mash.

On 1 November we were relieved by the Rangers. I accordingly left the cookhouse at about 1pm and went along to 'Dead End Post' where I picked up the other cooks and together we ambled down on our own from the line. After stopping at an estaminet on the way down we eventually arrived at our old billet in Laventie, and there we waited to make tea for the Company when they arrived later. As we had been in the line and so could not celebrate Hallowe'en in a fitting manner, it was decided to do so during our spell of rest. A Battalion dinner was held and to us fell the task of preparing the feast. All the cooks in the Battalion worked together and to 'D' Company fell the lot of preparing the Haggis and boiling onions. We cooked the Haggis in a big bath tub. The dinner took place at 3.20pm and the menu was:

> Soup
> Roast Beef and Onions
> Haggis
> Plum Duff and Syrup
> Dessert

This was followed by a Battalion concert for which we made rum punch.

On 3 November the sixteen members of the Company with the longest service had orders to parade at 8pm. I was amongst the number, so duly paraded at the appointed time. There was obviously something in the wind, and we scented a practical joke. One by one we had to appear before the Regimental Sergeant Major, our own Company Sergeant Major and Company Quartermaster Sergeant. The three endeavoured to give an official touch to the parade by asking us sundry questions as to the number of months we had been out in France etc. The Company Quartermaster Sergeant then said that it gave him much pleasure in the Name of Her Most Gracious Majesty Queen Alexandra to present us with a small present as a reward for our loyalty. At the command of 'forward Corporal Davidson' that gentleman handed us a parcel. The RSM shook hands with us, also on behalf of the Queen and the proceedings ended with a drink all round.

On 5 November the Battalion moved into the trenches again to relieve the Rangers, and we cooks went with the Company as before, but this time in advance. 'Tich' Davidson stopped at the 'Red House' (Battalion Headquarters) to collect the dixies from the Platoons as they passed later, and the rest of us went to 'Hougemont Post' to the position that the 'C' Company cooks had taken up after their cookhouse further up the line had been blown in by shellfire. We found that two boilers known as Sawyer Stoves had been installed, and while I was getting these into action the other two cooks went back to the 'Red House' to help Davidson bring along the dixies. We had got everything ready, when the CSM came along and told us we were to move further up the line. We passed along a communication trench called 'Edgware Road', and across another trench called 'Park Lane', until we reached 'Rotten Row', our destination. Trench boards had been laid about nine inches above the bottom of the trenches, but even then the trench in parts was flooded with water. After we had got our feet thoroughly soaked, and Macpherson had gone in over his knees, we decided to walk along the top of the trench and in the open. When we got to our new position a sorry spectacle presented itself. 'D' Company HQ was in a village which was absolutely smashed to smithereens. There was no sign of a billet, but at length we stumbled across a small room in a shell–battered house, occupied by two of 'D' Company's Lewis gunners. We then returned to bring our tackle along, and to do this we borrowed a truck from the REs. We had to make about ten journeys to get our tackle to this truck, and when we had finished loading we had to toil like the Israelites of old pushing it along a miniature railway track known as the 'Great Central Railway', for about twenty minutes. We then came to the spot where the track had been blown away by a shell. The Germans turned a machine gun on us, and we spent a very uncomfortable time. We unloaded and while 'Mac' and Davidson pushed the truck back to the terminus, Kerr and I, with the aid of two Officers' batmen took the dixies along to our billet. The next day we carried on our duties as usual. We had to be careful not to make any smoke, as that promptly drew the enemy's fire. During the morning we endeavoured to make the billet as comfortable as possible.

At 5.30pm we went with a party to the railhead to draw the Company's meat and vegetables etc. To do this it was necessary to walk about six hundred yards along the road, which was particularly unsafe after dark, for the Germans occasionally swept it with machine gun fire. They were busy that night very close to us, but our particular portion of the road did not claim their attention, at any rate not for the time that we were walking along it. When we got back we turned into our billet and read during which time we could hear the bullets battering themselves against the wall in front of us. I learned later that the name of the village was Tilloy.

The next day there was a very cold wind blowing and, as our cookhouse was exceedingly draughty, we set about blocking up the holes made by shells, with timber and sandbags. When the rain came on, however, the place was hopeless, for the water very soon came through the roof in miniature showers, and pools of water collected everywhere. Disaster faced us at night, for our sleeping apartment failed at the critical moment. The portion of the roof we had repaired was all right, but everywhere else through the roof streams of water came down. We put dixies and mess tins to collect it, but the whole floor with the exception of a small part where three of us slept, was very sooned turned into a quagmire. With the pressure of the continual rain part of the earth on and around the room came hurtling down, and we began to wonder how long the roof would hold before it came crashing down on us. So we were forced to look elsewhere for shelter.

We had now to turn to forbidden ground, namely an artillery observation post. This was a small dugout, made of sandbags and corrugated iron, but we could not lie down, for although the roof kept the water out, yet for some reason that was not apparent, the floor was covered with about an inch of water. There was nothing for it, therefore, but to sit up all night. Each of us took a dixie from our cookhouse to use as a seat and, with our feet on a board and a blanket round us, settled down to read by the light of a candle until daylight. About 10pm some batmen in another little hutch had orders to go up the line, and so we shifted our quarters to their abode. There was an inch or two of water on the floor, but we were able to sleep on floating boards. It certainly was damp, but despite that I was able to get a

98

good sleep.

On the 9 November the Battalion was relieved by the Rangers, so while Macpherson stayed behind to come along later with the Company, the other cooks and I moved down to Laventie in the morning, and when the Company arrived at 5pm we served up dinner. After four days we went back to the trenches again to take over from the Rangers. We cooks again separated, and I went with my Platoon to Picantin Post. We spent a fairly quiet time for a week, and then the Rangers came back and relieved us, and we went back to Laventie.

After many months of longing and weary waiting, my name at last appeared in Battalion orders for leave, so that when I went up with the Battalion to the trenches I went prepared to leave at a moment's notice. This time we took over 'B' Company's old position in the front line trench. There were two cookhouses, one of which was in the front line itself, with the comforting feeling that the Germans were very close and practically neighbours; the other was in the flank post. Our sleeping accommodation was in the front line trench, and consisted of two tiny shelters above ground, into which we could just crawl. A special feature of the billets was the rats, and in fact the whole area was infested with them.

On 26 November, after a wait of seventeen months, my orders arrived for leave, and at 2.30pm I joyfully set off for the Battalion Orderly room for my leave warrant. From there I went to Laventie where, with Macpherson and a fellow named McDougal, I went to an estaminet for a feed. After demolishing six eggs apiece, McDougal and I set off in good time to catch the train due at La Gorgue about 10.30pm.

We travelled down to Boulogne, where we alighted and marched to a rest camp. Later we embarked on board the *SS Onward* with light hearts and, after a crossing under the escort of a torpedo boat destroyer, landed at Folkestone at 2.30pm. We rushed to the waiting train like a crowd of maniacs. The whistle blew, the train drew out and later we steamed into Victoria Station. I was unexpected, and when I knocked at the door of my home and my folks opened it, and realised I had returned they advanced on me in sectional rushes. The first joy was a hot bath, with plenty of water. This was followed by a good feed with a knife and fork, implements almost forgotten.

My ten days' leave passed all too swiftly and on 7 December I had to buckle on my equipment and start back to France. My father and mother saw me off at Victoria Station at 6.15am. They showed a brave front, although I knew their feelings, and that helped me considerably, for heaven knows it was hard to part, and to be off again into the unknown with doubts as to what the future might hold for me.

On arrival at Folkestone I embarked on the *SS London* and eventually arrived at Boulogne, and at last found myself at a rest camp about a mile and a half outside the town, where I was put with nine others in a tent. Later in the day a party of us marched to Boulogne Station, and at 3pm left by train for the Front. I alighted at La Gorgue at 2am next morning. It was bitterly cold, and I set off to cover the four miles to Laventie. When I arrived I went to the Quartermaster's Stores and got down to sleep in a roll of blankets that I found there. When I got up next morning I found that Macpherson, Davidson and Sanders had also gone on leave, so that I was left in charge of three new cooks. The Company was in the trenches, but I was given instructions to stay at the Store until the Battalion came out of the line. I spent the time in cutting up meat, and in filling sandbags with coal etc., to be sent up on the ration limber. I slept at night in a farmcart standing in the Stores. On 10 December our Company Quartermaster Sergeant was unwell, so I went up to the trenches with the rations in his place. He was unwell again on the 12th so I made another trip with the rations.

On 17 December the Battalion returned from the trenches, but went back after five days.

When the Company were in the trenches, the cooker remained at the transport line, and two cooks stayed with it and daily cooked meat, bacon and vegetables, which were sent up to the trenches nightly with the rations. The other two cooks went up with the Company and made tea for the troops during the Company's spell in the line and also served out the rations. Then, on the next occasion, we used to reverse the role and the two cooks who had been in the line previously stayed with the cooker and the other two went up. We tossed up to decide which cooks should remain at the Quartermaster's Stores, and as I won I moved my kit to the Stores while the others went up to the trenches.

The weather was intensely cold, and the cutting of the meat was a tough proposition. It was frozen hard, as though we were chipping granite. I went up to the 'Red House' with a limber full of waterproof capes for the Battalion, and returned with a load of empty petrol cans.

On 18 December all 'D' Company's cooks had returned from leave, so that we were working with our original staff again.

Three days later our Brigade, the 168th, was relieved by the 167th Brigade and the Middlesex Regiment relieved the 'Scottish'. The Battalion moved down to La Gorgue for Brigade rest, and I went on in advance with the cookers and the wagons carrying the stores. When we arrived we found that 'A', 'B', and 'C' Companies' billets were together and that poor old 'D' Company was almost outside the town. When the Company arrived from the trenches we served up dinner and tea. We spent Christmas Day at La Gorgue. It was raining hard, and the mud around our cookhouse was appalling. There was very little excitement, for it had been decided to hold the Christmas festivities next day. We all had rather a bad attack of the 'blues', so we went to an estaminet in the evening in order to derive from it what little cheer we could, and later turned in. Personally I was not sorry to get down to it, as I had a pretty sore throat, and was feeling quite bad.

Our Christmas dinner consisted of stew! and a pudding from 'Blighty'.

There was an inspection by the Brigadier next day, and that was enough to mar any Boxing Day!

There was a Company Dinner in the evening, which we prepared and which consisted of roast beef and Christmas pudding, backed up by fruit and drinks, bought out of Company funds. Someone managed to raise a tablecloth from somewhere. There was a concert in the billet of 15 and 16 Platoons. There was an inspection next day, followed by another the day after!

On 30 December breakfast was fixed for 5.30am. Macpherson and I were on duty, and this necessitated our turning out at 4am as the Company was fairly large, and breakfast used to take quite an hour and a half to prepare. We ourselves overslept, and did not wake up till 5.20am. My word we got some move on. There was no time to boil the water by the ordinary fire, so we laid wood and paper under it and, after having lit the fire, stood about fifteen yards away and fed it with petrol lifted from an Army Service Corps dump nearby. The flames rose about twenty feet and as they died down we threw more petrol on. I think I can safely say that we easily broke the record that morning, and breakfast was ready by the time the Mess Orderlies arrived. Some of them were late, and it was a treat to hear Macpherson

let fly at them, telling them that they were late and that we had been
kept waiting. They replied that they had overslept, but 'Mac' said
'that was no excuse'. We spent the passing of the old year in bed, as we
had to turn out early the next morning.

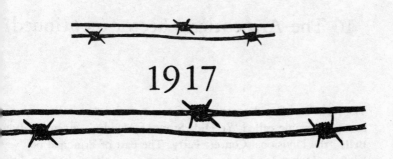

1917

16 The Armentières Sector (continued)

The New Year found us still at La Gorgue, and the next day we went to a pantomime called 'Ye Olde Story of Aladdin', given by 'Bow Bells', the Divisional Concert Party. The part of Principal boy was taken by Holland, a London Scot. It was an excellent show, and the dancing was really good.

The next day the Battalion again moved up the line. The cooks followed later and we found the rest of the Battalion at Pont du Hem. The cookhouse was very small, and so draughty that it was impossible to keep a candle alight. For the first time in two months, a different kind of jam was issued to us in rations. We had had plum and apple jam every day for two months, till we had got to absolutely hate the sight of it. The apricot that then appeared was therefore a welcome change. Our joy was short lived though for the very next day the detestable plum and apple again appeared on the scene.

After staying at Pont du Hem for seven days, we again got on the move and, on 9 January 1917, relieved the Rangers in the trenches. This time the Battalion took over a new sector of the line to the right of our old position. The cooks left just after dark with a limber and, after a weary journey over a road pitted with shell holes, we arrived at the ration railhead, known as 'Winchester Post'. There, a party was to have met us, but as no-one arrived I set off to the front line to get assistance. The communication trench was about sixteen hundred yards, and after I had covered this distance with my full pack I was very glad to get to our new position. The cookhouse was a little shanty, just behind the firing step, about ten feet by six feet, and in this there were firebars six feet long. When a fire was alight, the heat was terrific, and every time it was replenished it became necessary to retire outside until the smoke cleared away. When our dixies had been brought along we set to work, and about midnight issued tea to the trench sentries and fatigue parties that were at work. Of course we had the usual cookhouse callers and, what with them and the rations when they arrived, we could hardly move in our little shanty. However, about 2am the heat from the fire had died down, the last visitor had left and we were able to turn in. Two of the cooks slept on the floor, and Macpherson and I slept on a couple of trench boards. One of the trench sentries woke me next morning at 6am and well it was that he did so, for I felt as drowsy as anything from the heat.

On 11 January the Company was ordered to leave the front line, and to retire to a reserve trench, as the artillery were going to 'strafe' the Germans heavily. When they left, therefore, the only occupants—the sole defenders of the front line—were three Lewis gunners, a corporal and four cooks. Hardly a very warlike combination!

The next day the Company were again ordered to withdraw to the reserve line during one of our 'strafes'. This time only the cooks were left in the front line, and the Germans paid us the compliment of shelling us. We came through the storm, however, with our honour still intact! After dark they suddenly let fly at us again with their guns. The shells burst closer and closer, and twice our little cookhouse nearly collapsed through concussion. One shell landed about ten yards from the door, and we had to make a hurried exit to the trench to avoid being buried. Snow began to fall heavily and, on waking one morning, we found that it had drifted into the cookhouse, and the floor was covered. The weather also turned bitterly cold. The Rangers relieved us on 15 January and at 10am Davidson and I had orders to report to Battalion Headquarters. We set off, therefore, but finding water in the trench, decided to go on top and in the open along the ration railway track. No-one was allowed to go that way in daylight, as the track was under the observation of the Germans. There was a film of ice all over the sleepers, so that we were very lucky to come a cropper only once each. We lost ourselves, but eventually arrived at Battalion Headquarters, where with two cooks from each of the other companies, we set off down to Pont du Hem.

We found 'D' Company cookhouse, a small room with no windows, in an old farmhouse. After indulging in eggs, we made up the fire and waited for the cooker to arrive at the transport line. Later, when the Company got down from the trenches some hours later, we made tea for them, and then turned in for the night when we took off our boots for the first time in six days. We remained at Pont du Hem for six days, during which time a good deal of snow fell and on 21 January we returned to the trenches. The Company Sergeant Major wanted a cook to go up the line in advance with a party, so at 1.30pm

I set off. The 'Scottish' were the Battalion in reserve, and our new position consisted of a system of trenches and dugouts in an open field. There was an old farm which had been heavily shelled, and in and about this 'D' Company was billeted. The cookhouse was a corrugated iron erection and, although not at all shell proof, or even splinter proof, was quite comfortable. There was a sandbagged shelter adjoining, with room for four to sleep in.

When the rations had arrived, and we had served tea to the Company, we were glad to turn in to get a little warmth. We spent five days in that positon, during which the cold gradually grew more intense. One morning when Davidson and I got up to make breakfast, we found everything frozen. The lids were tight on the dixies, and our bread was as hard as rock. A pot of syrup was as solid as toffee, and we had to break the ice of the neighbouring stream to obtain water. We grew accustomed to the cold at last, but it was a painful process. As the days went on the cold got more intense. On one occasion I took a dixie of boiling water off the fire and stood it six feet away from the blaze, and within half an hour the water was frozen hard. The tea in our mugs became a solid mass; and we began to realise the hardships of a winter campaign!

I felt the cold tremendously on account of the fact that I wore exactly the same clothing in winter as in summer. I never wore a vest because of the vermin, for the little bounders did not need the slightest encouragement.

There was a gas alarm one evening, for the Germans had been observed bringing up gas cylinders. Soon after, gas was encountered in our front line, and so we had to put on our gas masks, and the whole Company 'stood to' ready for any trouble that might brew.

On 28 January the Brigade was relieved by the 167th Brigade. This was relief in every sense of the word, for the cold by this time had become well nigh unbearable. That morning we found ice three inches thick in our washing tin, and the meat when dropped sounded like granite.

After we had issued tea, Macpherson and I set off down the line. We had to wait for two and a half hours shivering in a biting wind for the limber to arrive, but as soon as this appeared we threw all the dixies etc., on board, and set off behind it. After walking for three hours we got to La Grande Pacart, a small village just outside Merville. The other two cooks had gone down in advance, and we found them in the cookhouse, a lean-to erection adjoining a barn. The Company was billeted in wooden huts, and we had places allotted to us in one of them. Each side of the huts was lined with bunks, and so we felt as if we were at sea. The weather was still bitter, and there did not seem to be any signs of a break. We moved our billet twice, first to a hut recently occupied by the Sergeants, and then to a barn adjoining a cottage. We moved the cooker to an outhouse nearby in which there was an oven. Things brightened up then, for there was plenty of straw in the barn to sleep on. The old gent in the cottage took quite a fatherly interest in us, and used to look after our fire and bring us cups of coffee.

The Brigade was out of the trenches for a twelve day rest, but after six this was cut short, so that on 2 February we had to move up the line again. We started off behind the cooker about midday, and after a fairly long march through Lestrum and Vieille Chapelle, we arrived at Croix Barbée shortly after the Company. About a mile before entering the village, the transport had to open out into artillery formation, with intervals of two hundred yards between each limber, in case of possible shellfire. Our cookhouse was in a farmhouse which had been pretty severely battered by shellfire. Our sleeping quarters consisted of a little room in which, by skilful manipulation, five of us could lie down. We found some straw mattresses and these, together with a fire, made things quite cosy.

The next morning the cold was still severe, and some of the fellows in the Company came round to our fire to get their boots thawed out.

When I went to wash I found my towel a solid lump, capable of standing up on its own, and in fact I walked round the billet using it as a walking stick! The hairs of my toothbrush were as hard as the handle.

After a stay of a week we packed up and moved off again. We were up at 4am and after packing a limber with our cooking tackle marched to a spot known as 'La Bassée Dump'. There, the limber was unloaded and all the things were put on some trucks on a light railway, and just before dawn we pushed the trucks to a new position that rejoiced under the romantic title of 'Moggs Hole'. It was situated behind the reserve line ('B' Line) and a few hundred yards in front of us we could see the battered ruins of Neuve Chapelle. As daylight had dawned we were unable to return the trucks for the track was under enemy observation. We shared a cookhouse with 'A' Company Cooks, and as it was impossible for eight of us to work at the same time we decided to do a spell of twenty four hours on and twenty four hours off. There was a little sandbagged shelter to sleep in, and when a brazier was alight the heat was absolutely unbearable. Four of us could barely lie down to sleep, and as the roof was only about four feet from the ground we had to go outside into the icy cold for a breather occasionally. The general position was by no means healthy, for all day long there was the whizz of shells over our cookhouse, and the nerve-wracking burst of shells from a giant trench mortar on our left.

The next night the Germans raided our front line, but received a very warm reception and they were beaten off, leaving a prisoner in our hands.

On 10 February our own artillery commenced to bombard the Germans just as the rations arrived. The enemy very soon retaliated, and shells and pieces of shrapnel came flying over and around our dugout. The excitement lasted for half an hour, and then gradually died down. The next day the Company left the reserve trench, and relieved 'A' Company in the front line. We made meals as usual, and these were carried up to the boys in iron containers. These were lined with asbestos to keep the heat in, and were slung with straps on the back of the carrier.

We made up a tremendous coal fire in the cookhouse. There was such a reek of smoke that everybody 'got the wind up'. An Officer came along, and ordered us to reduce the smoke. The trench mortar battery fellows who had their gun quite near to us got terribly alarmed, telling us that they did not want to draw the enemy's fire, as there was a big aminol dump near.

A sudden thaw set in, and everywhere in consequence became very slushy so that, if anything, conditions were worse than during the severe frost.

On 13 February the enemy again set about us with their giant trench mortars. I was hauled out of bed at 1am to go to the Company Sergeant Major's dugout to receive orders for the morning. I returned to my own dugout and was out again at 4.30am to make breakfast. The Company left the trenches, and I remained behind with another cook, and at 7pm we loaded our tackle on ration trucks on the light railway, and started off, pushing the truck down the line. When we had got a little way we met a party of Royal Engineers with six loaded trucks coming up. As it was only a single track we had to push our truck back to a siding to allow the others to get by. When they had passed we set off again, but had not gone far before we met another truck going up the line. We had three loaded trucks, so stuck our ground and refused to go back. Neither party would move, and we stayed there glaring at each other. At last the others decided to get their truck off the line, and we very willingly gave a hand in pushing it off. We then carried on until we arrived at a place called 'The Euston Dump' in the La Bassée road. There, a limber was to have met us, but it was nowhere to be seen, and we adjourned to a soup kitchen that we discovered there. Two hours later the limber arrived, and we loaded up and got under way for the reserve billets. After an hour and a half's stiff walking we arrived at the small village of Bout de Ville, where we found the cookhouse to be quite a good one with an oven and fireplace included. However, we were not to occupy it for long for there was an ear splitting shriek and a shell came whizzing through the air. This happened pretty frequently and, as the shells dropped on a farm very close to us, and threequarters of the Company were near, the area was considered to be unsafe for billeting purposes, and so we had orders to shift to the other end of the village.

The next day it turned very cold again, and when we went to shift the cooker we found the wheels frozen hard into the ground. The Germans put more shells over the old cookhouse, but ye birds had flown. A thaw set in again, and we worked in a veritable sea of mud.

On 19 February, a party of us went to the Divisional Baths at La Gorgue, and while we were bathing our clothes were fumigated, so that we had to wait for about an hour in only our shirts. I had had chronic neuralgia for two days, so this wait in the bitter cold did not improve matters.

On the next day the Battalion again went into the trenches. It was my turn to stay down at the transport line with the cooker so when the horses arrived at 10am I went down to the Quartermaster's Stores at La Gorgue. The cooks, one from each Company, were billeted in a barn next to the stores. Our duties consisted of cutting up meat, a job which took three hours, and in getting the rations ready to be sent up in limbers to the Battalion. I stayed at La Gorgue for six days, and on the 27th set off with the supply column to Croix Barbée, the village to which the Battalion came down from the trenches.

Whilst we were there a Battalion inspection was held. The Germans had been shelling the village severely all day and matters reached a climax when we were waiting to be inspected, for a building quite near to us was set alight by the shelling.

We returned to the trenches on 5 March, this time in the La Couture section.

Two cooks went up early with the limber containing our tackle, and Macpherson and I followed later with the Company. After a very roundabout march, lasting three hours, we arrived at the support line trench. The cookhouse was not so bad, although it was not high enough to allow us to stand up. The shelter in which we slept was small, about ten feet by five feet, and only three feet high. Five of us slept there, and we could only enter by crawling in on our hands and knees. We had to turn in one at a time, and when we were all in, we could not even turn. It was so dark that it was necessary to burn a candle night and day. We only remained in this section for four days, and on 8 March the Division was relieved and we were withdrawn from the line.

The outstanding feature of the Armentières sector was the extraordinary number of rats. The area was infested with them. At the rear of the trenches there were huge holes from which earth had been taken to fill the sandbags which formed the parapets. These holes filled up with water, and at night one could see the snouts of rats as they pushed their way across. It was impossible to keep them out of the dugouts even. They grew fat on the food that they pilfered from us, and anything they could pick up in or around the trenches; they were bloated and loathsome to look on. We were filled with an instinctive hatred of them, because however one tried to put the thought out of one's mind, one could not help feeling that they fed on the dead. We waged ceaseless war on them and, indeed, they were very easy prey because owing to their nauseating plumpness they were slow of foot. We would wait and watch for them as they left the water and climb awkwardly on to the boards at the bottom of the trench. Then with a run we would catch them squarely with a mighty kick, and there would be one less to batten on us.

The Officers on their nightly rounds would fire on them with their revolvers, and in the morning it would be a common sight to see disembowelled rats lying amongst our barbed wire.

We used to tie our food in sandbags, and these we would hang from a rafter of the dugout. The rats would get the food though, and to do that they must have climbed down the string.

One night a rat ran across my face. Unfortunately my mouth happened to be open and the hind legs of the filthy little beast went right in.

On another occasion a rat fell from a rafter just over the head of Robertson, the fellow who was sleeping next to me. 'Robbie' quickly closed his hand on his overcoat and the rat was caught and speedily finished off.

17 Arras

On 9 March 1917 the Battalion was relieved by the Duke of Wellington's Regiment, and about 9.30am we cooks went down to a place known as 'Sandbag Corner'. There we found a limber waiting, and on it we loaded our tackle and travelled down to Vieille Chapelle. The cooker, which had arrived from the transport line, was in a field, and we carried on making the dinner which was served up to the Company on their arrival later. We were on the move again next morning, soon after breakfast, and on arriving at Merville station we issued tea to the Company. The Battalion entrained, and left at midday, while Sanders and I travelled by a later train with the transport.

There were ten of us in a truck, together with eight heavy draught horses. There were four horses at each end and we were in the middle. Things looked fairly promising—but, oh, what a night we had! Soon after the train started the horses became restive, and at every jolt of the train there was a commotion. Every now and then one of the animals would stretch out his neck and 'playfully' try to catch hold of one of us by the ear, or of anything handy. After one especially severe jolt one of the horses fell down, and as they were closely packed it was only with great difficulty that it was possible to get it on its feet again. The drivers ran by the side of the train and picked up flints from the ballast. They threw these on the floor of the truck, but this proved of no avail, and blankets had to be placed under the animal's feet. Just as this horse was on its feet again, another animal fell over, and at this point the only candle alight in the truck was knocked over by another enterprising beast. Pandemonium reigned, and a stampede seemed inevitable. We, who were not in charge, took refuge on the footboard outside the truck. The drivers set about the animals, and eventually restored quiet. I got back into the truck, and settled for a snooze and, except for one or two further commotions during the night, nothing untoward happened.

We drew into Doullens next morning at about 8am and after the transport had been unloaded we set off to join the Battalion. After

112

travelling for about eight miles we arrived at Le Souich. The next day we moved on for another three miles to Ivergny.

It rained heavily next day, so we pulled the cooker under a straw shelter and there it stood in about six inches of slimy mud. Our sleeping place was small, so we cleaned out a pig sty thoroughly and had our meals there. While we were at Ivergny there was a Company Concert, for which we made rum punch. Davidson ('Tich' as we called him, or Cyril, as his fond parents christened him) volunteered to go and fetch the cooks' share of the rum punch. This was a mistake on our part to let him do it, for it put too a great a strain on his will power! 'Tich' was gone a long time—far too long for our peace of mind. He returned at last, distinctly elevated, and decidedly argumentative. He came back with our rum punch all right, but it was not in the bottle he took to get it in! No doubt 'Tich' meant well, but all the same we decided, in future, we should not send him for our share—at any rate not without escort.

The Battalion remained at Ivergny for twelve days, and on 23 March we set off on the move again. A march of ten miles over atrocious roads brought us to the village of Gouy en Artois. There the cookers were placed on the top of a hill and, by George, it was bitterly cold. The Battalion was in huts in the same field, but farther down the hill. It rained heavily one morning, and I spent a hectic time frying about a hundred rashers of bacon, with rain pelting down on the frying pans.

Mention should be made of the latrines at this place, for they constituted a hazard. A trench about eight feet long, three feet wide and about six feet deep was dug right on the brow of the hill. Across this a telegraph pole was supported at each end and on a breezy day one had the greatest difficulty in keeping one's balance without falling to a sticky end!

On 27 March the Battalion left Gouy, and marched by a very circuitous route to Agny, a suburb of Arras, which had been very badly knocked about by shellfire.

Preparations for another advance were obvious, for the place was alive with guns, and the Arras road was literally alive with 9.2 howitzers and naval guns. Our hopes of being billeted in the town itself were shattered, for we were marched to a line of dugouts outside, situated in a sunken road. We found a fairly roomy cookhouse, with a little dugout to sleep in, and returned to guide the cookers to our new positions, but found the way blocked by a column of motor lorries which had temporarily parked in the sunken road. We had to wait for over two hours, shivering in the cold, before the lorries pulled out. As it was dark by then I had to guide the driver with a flash lamp.

The village was shelled next day, and 'A' Company had forty casualties.

On 1 April 1917 our anti-aircraft guns brought down a German plane. The first shot hit it direct, cutting off one of the wings completely. The plane fell from a tremendous height, the wing fluttering down some time after, like a piece of paper. The same day about 3pm we followed the Battalion to Archicourt, a village about three miles away. The place had also been severely damaged by shellfire. Our billet was not so bad, though, for it was a small room in what had evidently been a small cottage. 'Tich' Davidson put glass in the windows, upon which piece of work the rest of us passed very sarcastic comments, because every time our guns went off the windows gave an aggravating rattle. Still, it kept the draught out, and that was the main object. ('Tich', I need hardly say, owed his nickname to his diminutive stature; he told us that he had been born in India, near Karachi, so that we sometimes used to call him 'The Nabob'. At times he was somewhat incoherent when Macpherson used to tell him to spit it on the wall and we will read it!).

On 3 April we moved up with the cooker for a distance of about a mile to some support trenches near the railway outside Archicourt. The cooker was drawn up behind a hedge to be out of sight of the enemy's observation balloons. The billet allotted to us to sleep in was about seventy yards away, and to get to it we had to climb over barbed wire, jump trenches and so forth. On getting there we found that the billet had been given to 'B' Company so that we were more or less homeless. At last we found an isolated house which had escaped the worst of the shelling. There we had a cellar to sleep in although it was a tight squeeze when we had all 'turned in'. The cooker was removed from its position from behind the hedge, and taken to our new billet.

The next day there was a great deal of aerial activity and one of our planes was shot down by a German plane about three hundred yards above our heads. The machine gun bullets were whizzing round and the British plane had a bad smash, turning over when about ten yards from the ground, and landing upside down. Later on, a German plane was forced to descend, and fell to our left in Arras. During the morning the area round the cooker became very hot. We were standing in the door of our billet watching the German shells bursting in the fields opposite, when there was a terrific crash and a shell landed in the road not half a dozen yards away. In a twinkling we scattered, and retired to the cellar.

On Good Friday (6 April) our guns were blazing away, and 'Fritz' replied with a vengeance, and rained salvo after salvo into Arras. At times spurts of flame showed where fires had been started by the shelling. They peppered Archicourt as well, and on several occasions we had to dart hurriedly to our cellar. The next day a line of tanks crawled slowly by on their way up to the scene of action. The night seemed alive and it was an awesome feeling standing there on the eve of a mighty attack in which the British alone were to send seven armies into attack at the same time. Our artillery was engaged in an intensive bombardment battering down the defences of 'Telegraph Hill' and Vimy Ridge.

On Easter Sunday the Germans turned their attention to Archicourt. Shell after shell burst in the village. Everything occurred at a most inopportune time for the village was filled with ammunition lorries. The square was packed with them, and a German shell caught a lorry full of 9.2 shells. There was a terrific explosion from the lorry which set light to the others, and altogether about half a dozen lorries were blown to bits. Men ran in all directions, and of course casualties were heavy. Everywhere one could see the debris of brick and woodwork, and the curled up chassis and bonnets of lorries. One chassis was blown completely up in the air, and landed on a housetop, and a wheel was found over a quarter of a mile away. Houses and men were blown to pieces beyond all recognition. Hours after the shelling had ceased dumps were exploding and going skywards.

Later in the day the Battalion moved up for the coming 'push'. We packed the cooker and, after having despatched it to the transport line, we donned our equipment and marched towards the scene of battle. Just outside Beauraines we joined 'A' and 'C' Company cooks. There we had to wait to make tea on their cookers for the boys before they 'went over the top'. Our guns were going strong putting the finishing touches. At about 1am we made tea, and soon set off with this in the asbestos chambers of the cooker limber to Beauraines, a village lying just behind the scene of the forthcoming battle. From there we carried the dixies of tea up to the troops. We had to pass through the village, and there a spectacle of havoc met our gaze. We had got to about the middle of the village when the Germans started to shell. We got through all right and arrived at the sunken road which we walked along for about a mile and a half. A German machine gun was turned on the road at intervals, and then we had to lie low and crouch down over the dixies of tea. We found the Company at last in a trench, and when they had had the tea we started off back with the empty dixies. We lost the other three parties of cooks so, getting 'fed up' with waiting, we 'D' Company cooks set off on our own. When we reached Beauraines about 4am the limber which was to have carried the dixies back was nowhere to be seen. We were thoroughly exhausted, but there was nothing for it but to carry on to the transport line. We met a fleet of tanks going into action, and then our trouble commenced, for we stopped to have a talk with one of the drivers and by so doing took the wrong road. We did not realise this until we walked into a strange village. After making some enquiries about our route we sallied forth again.

We now had trouble with 'Tich' (Davidson) for while we had been enquiring our way that obstinate warrior had dumped his dixie in the road declaring that he would not budge another inch—and when 'Tich' said that we knew by experience that even a salvo of shells would not move him. His language was if anything, stronger than his determination. The only way to deal with him was to tell him not to do a thing, and he would straightaway do it. With a sly wink to each other, therefore, we strongly advised him that as he was so done up it would be better not to move. This worked the trick, for with further lurid language he declared that he would be damned if he was going to stay there. Off we started again, therefore, still carting those confounded dixies. We walked for what seemed miles, and then found ourselves in a perfect hornet's nest of belching guns and, to our astonishment, found that we were in Arras, and moreover in that particular part that had been so unmercifully shelled the previous day. We did not linger by the wayside, but pushing on speedily by the railway station, another very unhealthy spot, found ourselves to our relief on the Archicourt road. A touring car came along, and we stopped it and asked the driver to give us a lift. He informed us that we had only a few hundred yards to go. We were so exhausted, however, that we could not even summon up sufficient strength to cover the short distance. We flung the dixies into the car, and struggled in ourselves, and in this manner arrived at the crest of the hill, on which we found the transport. It was then 6am and the great attack was just beginning, so we lay down and watched. Just as the grey streaks of dawn spread over the horizon, myriads of glistening lights burst forth—the many coloured star shells, the artillery signs of both combatants. After waiting for a time we struggled into camp, where we crawled into a dugout and were soon fast asleep.

The Battalion broke through the Hindenburg Line at 7.30am and carried on through the village of Neuville Vitasse.

At 5pm Sanders and I went up with a limber, which needed four horses to pull it because of the mud. We started off in a snow blizzard and stopped at Archicourt on the way to pick up fuel at the Quartermaster's stores. The road was very congested, as everywhere was blocked by the cavalry and big guns moving up. As we passed Beauraines we could see horses lying dead by the roadside and also wrecked ammunition limbers. We arrived at the trench from which the Battalion had attacked that morning and waited there while the Sergeant cook went off to get orders. We could see the effect of the shelling on the German trenches, and in places all semblance of a trench had been obliterated. By the roadside there were over thirty of our own men laid out on stretchers in their last long sleep. There were disabled tanks, and in all directions groups of Cavalry waiting to break through.

Later we moved up to a spot just outside Neuville Vitasse, where a party met us to carry the cooking tackle and we went with them through the village. Progress was very slow, for the road was congested with guns and ammunition columns. The Germans shelled us, but we managed to get through unhurt. We carried on over the German front line to their second, and at last arrived at their third line trenches. There we took up our quarters in a German dugout, in the occupation of our Company Headquarters. The dugout was thirty feet deep, and had three separate compartments, capable of holding fifty men. It was past midnight, so I curled up in a corner and went to sleep. Next morning I went up into the trench above and, after making a fire there, prepared to make tea for the boys. About seven yards away from me lay the dead body of a German. He was a hefty fellow and had been shot in the head, and his brains were spattered over his face.

The cookers were sent up from the transport line, and Sanders and I went back to the village to find them. In the daylight we could see the havoc wrought by our own guns in the village. It was terrible. What had been a flourishing village was now merely a heap of bricks. We could see where many a poor fellow had died fighting, and among them we recognised some from our own Regiment.

As we could not find the cookers, we returned to our dugout. The cooker arrived at last, but we were ordered to go back with it immediately. We joined the rest of the Company cooks at the trench from which the Battalion had attacked. We got everything unpacked, but we had no sooner done so than we were ordered to move again. We repacked, and moved to another position only two hundred yards away.

The snow began to fall, and everywhere was soon mud and slush. We made a shelter over the limber pole, and crawled under for the night, and what a night! The snow turned to rain, and where we were lying became a pool of water. Next a strong biting wind sprang up, and I did not sleep a wink all night, for the cold was perishing. It was with absolute relief that I at last saw daylight dawning. We got up and endeavoured to dry our sodden tunics and overcoats. The rain fell all day and the cold was intense, and in addition there was mud everywhere. In the midst of all this there was another move. Again we packed up, and by this time everything was covered with mud and slime. We passed through Neuville Vitasse and drew the cookers into a road near the dugout by which the dead German was lying. The mud in the roadway was thick and in places came over our knees. One of the horses in 'C' Company cooker fell down. It was a beautiful animal, but although a heavy draught horse, it had not sufficient strength to rise, and the mud gradually sucked it down. All efforts to raise it proved to be of no avail, although the poor beast made frantic efforts to rise. It was blocking the way of an ammunition column, so the Officer in charge of the column came up and shot the horse, and the column passed over its dead body.

We struggled on through the mud, and when we got to the dugout we practically dropped from exhaustion. Later we moved further up the line, and took up our quarters in another dugout with the Company. The Battalion then went further up and we stood by all day with the horses, in case we were needed. Later, however, we received orders to return to the transport line at Neuville Vitasse.

On 16 April the Battalion was expected to return, and we waited up all night for the men. We spent the time sitting in a large shell hole, over which we had spread our limber cover, but they did not arrive until 9.30am next morning.

The Germans shelled the guns near us and pieces of shell flew around us. At midday the whole Battalion had to 'stand to' as a German attack was expected. The gunners also stood ready, but luckily there was no attack. The weather was very severe, and alternated between rain, snow and biting winds.

At last on 19 April, we were relieved by the 18th Manchester Regiment. Just as we left to go down the line there was a terrific explosion, and an ammunition dump went up in the air. An anxious moment followed while the pieces from it came down to earth, but fortunately no one was hit. The roads on the way back were in a fearful condition, due to the heavy lorry traffic. Beauraines which was unsafe and deserted when we passed through only ten days previously, was now comparatively safe, and presented a lively scene, for everywhere there were horse lines, lorries and troops.

We staggered into Arras, smothered from head to foot in mud, and got settled in a billet in the Rue Lamartine in a timber yard littered with drain pipes, marble and tessellated tiles. After ten days of hardship in the open air, we once more had a roof over our heads. We had a gentle reminder that the Germans were not extinct, for just as we turned in for the night they started to shell Arras.

It seemed an irony of fate that now that we were back in billets the weather should clear up! To break the monotony even more, after living on Army biscuits for a fortnight we again received bread in rations.

Two days afterwards we were taken in motor lorries to Couin, near the Hébuterne sector and from there we marched to Coigneux. The cooker, which went by road, arrived later.

Our old skipper Captain Anderson rejoined the Company, and on the third day of our stay, during which the weather was glorious, we marched on another ten miles to Gouy, and again had our cookhouse on the hilltop. Camp was as bleak as ever, despite the warm weather.

We took the first opportunity of getting a bath and managed to indulge in one in the village of Gouy. We needed them badly, for after knocking about German dugouts, and living in the open without taking off our clothes for so long, our shirts were literally alive with vermin. The little bounders fairly gave us hell, and we were really glad to be able to don new shirts.

On 26 April we pushed on again, this time to Simoncourt, where the whole Brigade was billeted in corrugated iron huts. After a short stay, we moved up into Arras, eight miles further. We cooks were billeted in what had evidently been a swagger town house, Number 1 Rue Chancy, the residence of a M Paul Bellier, an agricultural implement maker. Our cooker was placed in a warehouse adjoining the house. All round lay barrows and other implements, twisted into various grotesque shapes by shellfire. The counting house and office had evidently been left in some haste, for everywhere there were strewn catalogues, office ledgers and the letter books of the business. To get the cooker into position a fatigue party was necessary to clear away the debris and fallen masonry.

We found an empty estaminet near the billet, and from there we 'borrowed' china plates, bowler hats and a homberg. We also scrounged some chairs, and so for the first time for months were able to sit down for meals. We used a fresh plate for every meal, and when we had done with it threw it into a corner. This labour saving method abolished the drudgery of washing up, and at the time we left there was a big pile of dirty dishes in the corner.

We discovered a small bicycle and rode round the square on it like a crowd of schoolboys.

Our sleeping quarters were 'posh' with parquet flooring, heating and electric light (but not working of course). There was also a fine marble fireplace, but despite this we lit our brazier and placed it in the centre of the room. On the wall hung a calendar from an English firm, Messrs Bentall and Company of Malden, Essex. At night we lay down to sleep under an artistically painted ceiling.

We found to our cost that our recent baths at Gouy had not been sufficient to free us from vermin. Everyone was alive with them and all day and night it was a question of scratch, scratch, scratch, until one's skin became absolutely raw. To make matters worse we had no spare shirts as, being continually on the move, it had been impossible for the Battalion to get a fresh supply.

We were only permitted to enjoy our luxurious bedroom for a couple of nights, for the Germans shelled us pretty badly, and as some of the shells burst very near we decided to shift to a wine cellar. Several artillery fellows were killed outside in the street, and a horse had its leg broken and had to be shot. In addition to the shelling, five German planes came over and bombed us.

Macpherson had a very bad attack of muscular rheumatism in the hands and feet, and was almost mad with pain. We fixed up an improvised bed for him in the cellar by taking a door off a cupboard and placing it on a stand upon which beer barrels had previously stood. We lit a brazier to give him warmth. Towards night he became absolutely raving with pain, and four of us took it in turns to watch him all night, rubbing his feet and hands every ten minutes. The Medical Officer gave him a morphia tablet, but the pain prevented 'Mac' from getting to sleep properly. The next day he was a bit easier, so we carried him up and made him as comfortable as possible in the sunshine. The following day the dressing station staff sent for him, and he was taken away to hospital.

On 3 May we moved to Tilloy, a little village two miles to the east of Arras, were we encamped in the open air. We dug an emplacement near the cooker over which we threw the limber sheet. We found later that we had struck a fairly warm zone, for very soon German shells came whizzing over too near for comfort. The animals on the horse lines close by had to be taken away during the 'strafe'.

About midnight the Company Sergeant Major came along and informed 'Tich' that he was to pack up immediately to go to Boulogne for a holiday. A new scheme had been inaugurated by which arrangements were made for parties of troops to go to a camp near the sea for a rest.

A big attack was scheduled for 5.30am and at 4am our bombardment commenced. The steady roll of the guns developed into an intense roar just before dawn. The Battalion moved up about a thousand yards to act as support for the attack, while we remained at Tilloy with the cooker.

On 11 May the Battalion went 'over the top' with the 4th Fusiliers, and succeeded in taking 'Cavalry Farm'. The 7th Middlesex Regiment had made a similar effort a few days previously, but had been beaten back.

We took up a new position on the Arras side of Tilloy, and then stretched a sheet over a shell hole in a wood and waited for the Battalion. The trees of the wood were badly battered, and the place was literally honeycombed with shell holes. We spent the night there in the rain, and early next morning the Battalion came down from the line. Shortly after breakfast we marched down to Arras and the Battalion, with the rest of the Brigade, was billeted in some French cavalry barracks called 'the Schram Barracks'. We stayed there for five days, and spent a fairly quiet time.

One evening I went to see a performance given by the 'Elegant Extracts', the 3rd Divisional concert party. The hall in which the performance was given was, no doubt, in peacetime the pride of Arras, but its glory was somewhat faded, for there was a great shell hole in one of the walls, and the rain percolated through the roof. However, we were an appreciative audience, and thoroughly enjoyed the star turn—'An Impression of Charlie Chaplin'.

Another evening we went to see 'Bow Bells', our own Divisional concert party.

On 19th May we set off on the road again, and left the Arras sector.

18 Simoncourt—Archicourt— Moule—Liencourt

After an easy march of seven kilometres we arrived at Berneville, and were billeted there in huts. We were only there for two days, but even in that short time two inspections were put into the programme. There was another move, and we found ourselves at Simoncourt. No billets had, of course, been set aside for the cooks, so we made a shelter in an adjoining orchard. We stayed at Simoncourt just a month for a rest. Battalion and Brigade sports were held, also boxing competitions, football, concerts, and unfortunately the inevitable inspections.

On 10 June we marched off to Montenescourt where we were put into an old barn for the night, and next morning pushed off again till we got to Archicourt about 8pm. The cookers came on later with the transport. One of the wheels of our cooker had collapsed, so that the cooking portion had to be left by the roadside outside Dainville, while the fore part joined us at Archicourt. A new wheel was sent down, and the stranded portion was brought on later. Just after breakfast next day a loud explosion heralded the arrival of a shell from a German 11ins Naval Gun. This landed in our Officer's Mess wounding our 'Skipper', Captain Filshall, and four batmen. All their cooking utensils were blown to smithereens, so we did the cooking for the Officers. The German plane that had been observing for the battery and had given us such a harassing time was shot down. When hit, it turned over and over and came to an ignominious end in Arras.

We spent nine days of glorious weather at Archicourt, and on 20 June the Battalion moved up to Wancourt to relieve part of the 167th Brigade. We were to stop at Beauraines while the Battalion was in the line, and on arrival there we found the transport in an open field thick with mud. There was not a vestige of shelter, and there was only a hour before darkness fell. We gathered sandbags and iron posts, and with these and the limber cover erected a small shelter just big enough for five or six to squeeze in. Hanson of Headquarters Company, was attached to us for a time.

After we had been at Beauraines for a fortnight all the Battalion cooks set off down to Archicourt. There we joined the cookers from the rest of the Brigade, and moved down to Liencourt, where we waited for the Battalion which arrived later in motor buses. A fortnight was spent at Liencourt, but the only event of any importance as far as the cooks were concerned was the formation of the League of the Red Triangle (red triangle was the Battalion sign worn on the sleeve of our tunics). The League was a society formed by 'D' Company cooks and had for its object the gathering together of its members to indulge in 'posh' feeds, and by so doing to keep up the spirits of the troops! The liability attaching to membership consisted of supplying the wherewithal upon which to feed. We held highly successful meetings—and our spirits benefited considerably!

On 22 July we marched for about six miles until we arrived at Buneville. Later that night the cookers left for the railhead and I was up early next morning to make breakfast, and at 4am left with the Company for Petit Houvin. There we entrained in the usual trucks (forty 'hommes' and eight 'chevaux'). We detrained at St. Omer and, as soon as the transport had been unloaded, we set off behind the Battalion. The heat was terrible, and my pack caused me agony. After marching for two and a half hours we reached our billets in the little village of Moule, just off the St. Omer road. The one thing that struck me most forcibly was the excessive politeness of the villagers. I heard later that a Highland Regiment had recently been billeted there, and that during their stay one of the fellows had rather ungraciously strangled one of the village maidens. This may, of course, have had some bearing on the civilians' politeness, especially as we ourselves were a kilted regiment, and for all they knew may have been thugs or stranglers.

After a few days we were obliged to shift our billet. This was not due to military pressure, but to the very strong aroma that came from the cowshed nearby. We had rubbed shoulders with many bovine friends in our travels, but the one in that shed was too much for us. We found another outhouse, which bid fair to be less 'ozony'. There was a pig in a sty about a yard away, but the odour from him seemed of a quieter variety.

I was picked with two others to go for a rest to Boulogne, so on 5 August we started off to join the train at Eperlecques about seven and a half kilometres away. We eventually detrained at Boulogne, and from there with a brass band heading the column marched gaily for about five kilometres to the 5th Army Rest Camp, just outside the little village of Equihen. We were put twelve in a tent, and after blankets had been issued settled down for a restful holiday. I spent twelve perfectly glorious days there. On 18 August our holiday, to our great regret, came to an end, and we marched to the station at Boulogne and there entrained for an unknown destination.

19 Ypres—Le Transloy—Lagnicourt

We arrived at a desolate little station in Belgium called Poperinghe. We detrained, and then marched for three hours till we arrived at a camp close to Ouderdom, where we found the Battalion in tents. There was no more room in any of the tents, so I dropped down beside the cooker which I found standing in a cornfield.

The Division had been in action at Ypres and had been severely cut up; one Battalion, the Fusiliers, had only fifty left. The 'Scottish' had been in reserve, but even then had had sixty casualties. The Division was so depleted in number that it had to be withdrawn from the line, so that we only stayed at Ouderdom for five days. Every night, though, during that time, the German planes visited us dropping bombs everywhere. We were in a cornfield all the time without any cover whatsoever, so we did not look forward to those nightly visitations.

On 23 August two of the cooks moved off with the cooker in advance, and I waited to march later with the Battalion next day. We left about 2pm for a station about a mile beyond Reninghelst and, after a journey averaging about four miles per hour, we reached Watton, and from there marched to our old billets at Moule. After five days we shifted again, and marched to Arques at such a rate that fellows collapsed in the ranks. We entrained there, and there were so many in my truck that I could not move. We sat with our chins touching our knees, and had to remain in that position for nine hours. We left the train in the early hours of the following morning at Bapaume. We spent the afternoon pitching tents for the 167th Brigade and then continued our journey for another three miles to some huts at Le Transloy, just near a sugar refinery. On 4 September the Battalion went up in support.

Macpherson, who had rejoined us, went back with the cooker to Fremicourt while I went up with the Company. The Battalion was lying in support in the village of Lagnicourt, and 'D' Company's position was in a sunken road to the left.

The village on our right was one mass of ruins, and looked like a deserted brick field. Our new cookhouse was a lean-to shelter with a trench fire made of rails. We slept in a corrugated iron and sandbag erection a few yards away from the cookhouse. While we had been carrying out the relief the Germans had shelled the village, and next morning they turned their attention to the sunken road, sending over salvos of 'Pipsqueaks'.

One man was killed and several were wounded, one of whom died later in the dressing station. We remained in the sunken road for six days during which the Germans shelled the village with 'Heavies' practically every day. Shells also fell round our position, but except for that we had a fairly quiet time.

On 10 September 1917 the Battalion relieved the Rangers in the front line and support trenches. 'D' Company were in the support line, and so as soon as it was dark, we moved off, with a fatigue party of twelve men to carry our dixies, through the village to another sunken road just beyond the crest outside the village. The road was thickly dotted with dugouts, and the cookhouse which we shared with 'B' Company was quite a 'posh' affair.

We arranged to work together in shifts, and by so doing were able to work twenty four hours right off the reel, and then to have forty eight hours off. This was, of course, quite unofficial, so that during our spells off we did not make our presence too evident. On 30 September, about 1am, there was a tremendous 'shindy' for Fritz was apparently attacking one of our advance posts. The night was a blaze of light on our left, and soon the order was passed along the sunken road that everyone was to 'Stand to'. The rest of the cooks who were in the dugout enjoying their forty eight hours off had to turn out and hastily dress (undressing, by the way, was strictly forbidden as we were so close to the Germans—nevertheless we always chanced it). One of 'B' Company's cooks was working with me, and we both got our rifles and equipment and then carried on with our job. The Germans shelled our position heavily all night. At last the excitement died down, and all was comparatively quiet on the Western Front!

The Rangers arrived on 16 September to relieve us and, after our limber had been loaded we set off for Fremicourt. We stopped at Beugny on the way down, and had tea at the YMCA hut there. We arrived at Fremicourt at midnight just as 'D' Company, who had travelled by the light railway, was detrained. We found the cooker in full steam with Macpherson and 'Tich' Davidson in attendance.

127

Next morning I could see our new position properly. We were perched on a high piece of ground which was, to say the least, very draughty. The Battalion was in tents along the Bapaume road, by the side of the light railway track. We remained there for six days, during which a party went to the Divisional Baths at Beugny. We sent 'Jock', our mascot, for a bath, and he came back the acme of cleanliness—and then spent the rest of the day by the cooker rolling on the top of a coal heap.

Although we were in such a desolate hole there must needs be an inspection, and everyone had to turn out, transport included. We marched to the parade ground, and at 10am the Corps Commander and all his satellites, great and small—mostly the latter—walked round us and peered at us as though we were some strange species. Their opinion of us was evidently fairly favourable, for shortly after we were marched back and dismissed.

Six days later we went back for another six days spell in the line. After a march of about three hours at a very stiff rate we arrived back again at the support line in Lagnicourt. The Company went on to the front line, and we cooks took over our old position with 'B' Company cooks in the sunken road to the right of the village. We again worked by turns, but this time in twelve hour shifts.

At dawn on 25 September there was a regular 'dust up'. The Germans bombarded our front line, and also the road in which we were. One of their bombing parties then visited our front line, and captured one of 'C' Company's men and we all had to 'stand to'.

During this time pandemonium reigned, and the air was filled with the bursting of 'Heavies', 'Minis' and machine gun fire. Just before actual daybreak the shelling died down, and all was quiet. The Battalion casualties numbered fifteen. There was further excitement for us in the afternoon when six German planes made a dash at one of ours. The 'Britisher' put on speed and made a beeline straight over our cookhouse, only about a hundred and fifty feet up. The enemy's planes opened on us with their machine guns, with the result that the bullets came whizzing through the air close to us. We retired to the cookhouse, therefore, and sat with our backs to the wall nearest the enemy.

The Rangers relieved us again on 27 September. As the Germans had taken a prisoner from whom they might glean information as to the usual time of relief, on this occasion the relief was altered, so that

128

we left the trenches a day earlier. We went into the support position in the sunken road to the left of Lagnicourt.

One morning four small red balloons came flying over the enemy's lines at intervals and were brought to earth by rifle fire. Each had a small bundle of newspapers attached, which contained news of the fall of Riga, and the casualties caused to the Belgian civilians by our raid, and also our casualties at Ypres. All very interesting, but if intended to put the 'wind up us' they were a miserable failure.

We spent six days in the sunken road, and then moved back to the other side of the village.

On 6 October we had to 'stand to' at midnight, while our artillery sent over gas from cylinders. These were fired from trench mortars from the front line, and a thousand in all were shot over to the Germans. We had to be prepared in case there was any retaliation, but after some time, as nothing happened, we received orders to 'stand down'.

There was a brilliant exhibition of red tape that night. At 1am we had to put our watches back to twelve midnight to conform with the provision of the Daylight Saving Act. Divisional orders also directed that we should 'stand to' for a gas stunt from 12pm to 1am. We 'stood to' for the required hour, and then thought that we had finished, but no, back went our watches to 12pm and so we had to obey Divisional orders again and do another hour's 'stand to'.

I got down to sleep at last at about 2am only to be up again at 4am to make breakfast, so that what with 'stand to's and time alterations, I lost heavily in the 'sleep stakes' that night.

On 8 October 'C' Company carried out a bombing raid on the German trenches, with the object of attacking the enemy holding 'Magpie's Nest', a little wood to the right of them. They blew up the wire in front, but were unable to get to the next two belts of wire, and so had to retire. They had four casualties, one of whom died later from wounds.

The Battalion moved up again later, but it was my turn to stay behind.

On 2 November Sergeant Baxter arrived from the line, and later I went with him to Fremicourt to take over the cookhouse of the camp to which the Company were to go, and there I waited to have tea ready for them on their arrival. The Battalion remained in the camp for six days, and there Hallowe'en was celebrated. We prepared the necessary dinner, and the more than necessary rum punch—two gallons of it. When we retired to the hut to sleep, we found the Company fellows decidedly elevated. One of them would persist in handing round lighted tapers and tablets of soap, although quite what relation the tapers had to the soap I was at a loss to fathom.

On 8 November our cooking tackle was packed on a Lewis gun limber, and we followed the Company to the trenches. We marched through Beugny and Monchy, and at the latter place branched off to a track. The mud was awful, and when we arrived at the sunken road in which our cookhouse was situated, we found the whole place congested with traffic. When rations arrived we unloaded them and helped to reload them onto pack animals. These then carried the rations to the various Companies in the trenches.

We got up next morning to find the door of the cookhouse absolutely blocked by a pile of trench mortar shells, and before we could enter we had to clear the whole dump away. We had trouble with the smoke problem, for the wood was wet and the fumes played havoc with our eyes and heads. Once when the 'fug' became too thick had to rush to the door, and was only brought round by vigorous thumps on the back that one of the cooks gave me!

On 14 November a party carried our dixies to the sunken road to the left of the village, and there the Company joined us. We were there for five days and then the Fusiliers (167th Brigade) came up and relieved us. When the limber arrived for our tackle in the evening we set off with it, and when we got to the mine crater at the crossroads we found a state of chaos prevailing. Our transport had met the Fusiliers transport, and neither column dared move for fear of falling headlong limbers and all, down the crater. No lights could be shown as the place was under observation by the Germans, and was a favourite target at night for shelling and machine gun fire. At length, by dint of prodding about with sticks, the passing was successfully carried out. We set off once more in the pitch dark; there were many shell holes, and we fell into most of them! Luckily, the rear half of the limber had a light coloured cover, so that we could just see it about a yard away, and so were able to make that our guide. We stumbled along into Monchy where we encountered many obstacles in the form of guns being shifted and heavy traffic. In fact there was obviously to be 'something doing' in the near future. At Beugny we found the Company billeted in huts (London Camp), which were spread about among the battered houses. We tried to get to sleep in one of the huts, though some of the fellows there were very lively, and required assistance in getting to bed.

An attack opened up in front of us, and on the stroke of 6.30am a bombardment started on our left flank. Very soon the sky was dotted with German Verey lights and red and golden flares. The infantry 'went over' when the barrage lifted. There ws no attack on our immediate front. All signs and indications, however, were made at Lagnicourt to give the impression that an attack was to be launched. Batteries of guns had been taken up each night, and taken away again before dawn. At daybreak smoke was sent over from the front line at Lagnicourt, and there were six tanks out in front, one real and five dummies made of light metal. Shortly after the bombardment ceased dummy figures dressed in tin hats and khaki tunics were made to pop up and lurch forward, as if in the act of going over the top. There were high powered motor cycles also in the front trenches to give an engine effect to the dummy tanks.

We waited all day ready to move up. Later, news came through that the dummy tanks and figures had been a success, for on first seeing them the Germans pummelled them unmercifully, and so wasted much good ammunition. The troops on both flanks went forward and, meeting with little resistance, advanced on all points. The distance gained varied from a hundred and fifty yards to five miles.

On 21 November the Battalion moved off at 7.30am to Beaumetz-le-Cambrai in battle order. The cooker could not go with them, as after leaving Beugny the road was under observation. We went down later to Fremicourt (Lock Camp); there, we stood ready packed, as we expected an order to rejoin the Battalion at any moment. Darkness fell and, as no order was received, we scrounged some blankets and turned in for the night.

The Battalion went into action the day after with slight casualties. They gained their objective, and took a hundred prisoners. The next day the enemy counter-attacked five times in force. The brunt of the fighting fell on 'A' and 'D' Companies, and they suffered heavily, losing all Officers and Sergeants except one. Captain Walker, our 'Skipper', was wounded and reported missing. In spite of all, however, the enemy were beaten off.

Next day the Battalion went back to the reserve trenches, and two cooks from each Company went up with a limber to make tea for them.

On 30 November the cookers were taken up to Beugny, and waited there for the Battalion. The boys arrived about 5am the next morning, and a sorry tale they had to tell.

The next night we were just getting down to sleep when the order suddenly arrived to get ready to move in half an hour. A staff Officer of the 51st Division arrived to take over the billets, and after a rush to be ready in half an hour we moved off three hours later.

We followed the Battalion, and after a march of about five miles over rough tracks arrived at Berlincourt.

20 Ecurie—Roclincourt—Vimy Ridge—Maroeuil

We woke up next morning to find ourselves in the grip of an icy cold December day, and we were faced with yet another move. However it was a move down, and so made all the difference. My feet were in a very bad condition so the 'Skipper' allowed me to strap my pack on his charger. After covering a distance of five miles we arrived at Beaulencourt, near Le Transloy, and there we took over some huts. The cold was still terrible, and there was a biting wind, and we simply shivered all day long. We stayed there for the night, and pushed on again next morning. For sheer discomfort, I think that a Division on the move takes some beating.

The Battalion marched off, and achieved a remarkable piece of military strategy, for after what seemed hours we arrived at Beugny—the place we had left two days previously! There we entrained, and four hours afterwards arrived at Beaumetz, and from here we had a march of about two kilometres to Simoncourt. This took us about an hour and a half for we progressed in bursts of about ten yards. The trouble was caused by being continually held up by the Divisional transport. This put the finishing touches to me and my groggy feet; when I arrived at the billet I could hardly move, and the next day I could hardly put my feet on the ground. Two days after, we moved on again. There was a long march before us, and neither Macpherson nor I were in a fit state to march, so the Medical Officer gave us a 'chit', allowing us to travel on the blanket lorry, and so we stayed behind when the Battalion moved off. The lorry appeared in the afternoon, and after it had been packed with blankets, we set off seated on the tailboard. As the lorry drew into Mont St. Eloi there was a shout of 'lights out'. The place was soon in pitch darkness, and the lorry was unable to move, so we remained in the road perched on the blankets on the top of the lorry. Overhead there was the whirr of an enemy plane, and soon there was a whizz, followed by a loud explosion, and a bomb damaged a camp nearby. When the invader had cleared off we got going again.

On arrival at Ecouvres we alighted, and then wandered all over the

place and at last found the Company in a big French hut in 'York
Camp'. There were about three hundred fellows in it on three tiers o
wire beds.

On the next night there was a Company concert, for which w
made rum punch, and if inebriation is any test, the concert was a hug
success! We moved on again, this time to Ecurie where we were agai
put into huts at 'Springvale Camp'. The Company went on to Bailleu
next day whilst the other three companies went into the support lin
behind the Kensingtons.

On 18 December the Battalion were relieved and so I moved u
with the cooker to 'Springvale Camp', Ecurie. The cold was sti
intense with a biting wind. We stayed in that camp for five perishin
days, and the cold froze one to the marrow. On one morning I foun
my boots frozen hard, yet in the midst of this bitter weather ther
must, of course, be an inspection! An inspection at the best of times i
an abomination, but in cold weather it is purgatory.

We got on the road again on 22 December for Roclincourt an
there we billeted in 'West Camp'. We were very comfortable, as eac
of us had a wire bed. As might be expected, it was for one night only
for the next day we continued our travels. We set off on a march, th
like of which I do not want to experience again. At first we walke
behind the Lewis gun limber, on which our tackle was loaded and w
carried on for about two miles till we came to the daylight railhead
There the limber was unloaded and the dixies etc., were handed to th
Platoons to carry. An endless march followed along a railway cutting
till we branched off on to duckboards and walked, and walked, an
walked. At last we came to a communication trench called 'Ouz
Alley', and along this we went for what seemed to be miles. It took u
well over an hour to get to the front line trench. As I was carrying tw
full sandbags, besides my pack, rifle and equipment, I felt might
glad when I was able to dump everything down in the cookhouse, an
sit down for a rest. There was a Sawyer stove and a trench fire in th
cookhouse, and so we set to work and made tea. There was no othe
outlet for the smoke but the doorway, and the 'fug and squash' wer
chronic. Our hours of duty ran from 4am till after midnight ever
day.

On the first day there was a gas alarm, for the Germans had starte
putting over gas shells and we had to make a dash for our respirators.

25 December dawned—a perfect Christmas from the Christma

ard point of view, for the snow lay thickly everywhere, but, alas!, the ast thing we wanted was seasonable weather. We did our best as far as ossible, to keep the Feast. Our resources were sadly limited, for we ad a dugout eight feet by six feet by five feet, absolutely reeking with moke. The already small floor space was still further reduced by sacks f fuel, tea and sugar. At every step we tripped over something, lespite the fact that we were always tidying up. Added to these roblems were the numerous cookhouse callers who pleaded to be able o sit by the fire and, as it was freezing outside, we had not the heart to urn them away. We received the usual Christmas greetings, but I egret to say that they fell on deaf ears, for reference to goodwill eemed distinctly inappropriate. We could not get much in the way of atables, as the canteen was practically sold out, so we made our Christmas dinner off Christmas pudding out of a parcel, and custard. After this we sat round with some of our pals, exhaling the fumes of igars, also out of parcels. We were quite happy considering the ircumstances, and could have remained so if 'Fritz' had not thought it to shell us at that particular moment. He sent some shells vhistling over our heads. There was a crash, and a shower of dust as a hell landed about ten yards from our door, and we had to make a dart long the trench, and one fellow was wounded. Things became uieter after a bit, so we returned to the cookhouse. Fritz started his ame again later, but luckily nothing came very near to us. Boxing Day was fairly uneventful. There was another heavy fall of snow, and owards the end of the day a sharp spell of frost. The enemy bumped s on and off all day, but our own artillery was to blame as they kept barking' at the Germans all day long. We were shelled again next lay, not quite so severely, but as I was expecting to go on leave at any ime I naturally felt anxious.

On December 28 the 3rd Fusiliers (167th Brigade) came up and elieved us. We cooks fell in with Number Sixteen Platoon, and stood hivering in the cold waiting to move off. Overhead there was an erial battle, and a German plane drove one of ours down. This was uite interesting until the machine gun bullets began to whizz round s. At last we set off down the never ending communication trench. The going was very difficult as the 'duckboards' were covered with ce. Just before leaving the trench we were held up, during which ime we were shelled heavily, and my vision of leave was gradually ading away. So near and yet so far. Yes, I had 'the wind up'!

On the second night after our arrival at 'Curragh Camp' Roclincourt, we visited the Divisional Canteen, and got in a stock Five of us then retired to a cottage and prevailed upon the old lady there to cook for us. We started with an omelette each containing ten eggs, with two large bowls of chips between us. We then knocked back two pounds of galatine of chicken and finished off with two pounds of chocolates, champagne and cigars. The evening was a huge success! Our return to the billet was quite a triumphal march. We had difficulty in getting one of the cooks along for he refused to walk, so we slid him along in the snow, sleigh fashion. We met an Officer on the way, and we had an awful job with our inebriate friend for he shouted out 'Why, there's old (mentioning the Officer's name)', and wanted to go and slap him on the back. Fortunately the Officer concerned was a sport and looked the other way. After a great deal of difficulty we at last got our friend to the billet. We all felt quite merry, and did not think it was such a bad war after all!

The next day I went to the Medical Officer to get my 'lice' ticket signed in preparation for going on leave. Everyone going on leave had to have a certificate stating that he was free from vermin and scabies. The ticket read:

I CERTIFY THAT 510803 . . . . . . RANK . Private . . . .
NAME DOLDEN A.S. . . . . 1st London Scottish

IS FREE FROM VERMIN

Signature of M.O. . . . . F.E. Mason . . . .
UNIT OR APPOINTMENT . . . . . Lt. R.A.M.C. . .
31.12.17.

Scabies I could understand, but how any MO in France could in all conscience ever say that a 'Tommy' was free from vermin was beyond my comprehension, since it was well nigh an impossibility. However I did not worry about that, and was only too glad to get the certificate.

1918

21 The Great German Offensive

On New Year's Day I started off on my second leave. I had only to wait about twelve months for this one, although it was quite long enough. After two hours' wait at Maroeuil station I entrained with the leave party. A cold journey followed, spent mostly in stamping one's feet in an attempt to keep warm, till we arrived at Boulogne. We marched to the 'Vidor Rest Billet' (the Old Fish Market), and spent the night there.

The next morning we sailed on the SS *Invicta* with the customary torpedo boat destroyer escort. After a breezy passage we disembarked at Folkestone, and eventually arrived at the 'Promised Land'— Victoria Station.

My leave was longer this time, but nevertheless it seemed to pass just as quickly. All too soon the end came, and on 16 January I had again to pack my grip and take a trip, but not to Tennessee, worse luck!

I arrived at London's Victoria Station in the early hours of the morning, but, on presenting my travel warrant to the Collector, it was discovered that the wrong half had been detached when I had arrived at Victoria at the start of my leave. Two members of the Military Police were immediately called, but as my explanation did not seem to satisfy them the 'Great White Chief', the Provost Marshall, was brought into the argument. After a lengthy discussion during which all my particulars were taken I was allowed through the barrier.

There was a sequel to this incident, for some time after my return to the Regiment, I received an official letter from the War Office referring to what had happened at Victoria Station. The missive ended by declaring that I was to be charged for my return fare to 'save the public money'! Needless to say I was furious because I felt that had I had been a deserter the public would have been put to far greater expense. I wrote a letter to *John Bull*, a periodical at that time that specialized in dealing with complaints. It was largely a matter of principle, as I realised that it would not have passed the censor and so of course there was little use in sending it.

I eventually arrived at Folkestone and boarded the *SS Victoria*. She was one of the slowest of the leave boats and we had a very rough crossing. At Boulogne we marched to a camp at the top of the hill, and the next day we entrained at Boulogne Station. There was a terrible crush, and I just managed to squeeze into a brake van. The speed was not excessive; in fact at one point the stoker of the engine was strolling along a little way in front of the train. Three trains travelled, one behind the other, at an interval of twenty yards. I detrained at Mont St. Eloi, and from there, together with another Scottish fellow returning from leave, travelled on a light railway for Roclincourt. At Bray we espied two of the 'Scottish' transport fellows so, as we were doubtful of finding the Battalion at Roclincourt in the dark, we decided to get off there. We found an old empty house in which two Pioneers were billeted, and decided to stop there for the night. By a stroke of luck we discovered a blanket store, so making up our minds that we would spend at least one warm night in France, we took twenty blankets each and settled down for the night. After breakfast next morning Smith, a Pioneer, and I put our packs and equipment in the Canteen cart and set off behind it. After three hours we reached the Battalion at Roclincourt. They were up to their eyes in mud in a place that was a picture of desolation.

On 24 January the Battalion moved off by train. Unfortunately, however, two cooks had to take to the road with the transport! We marched through Haute Avesnes, and at Savy Berlette stopped for an hour to rest and water the horses. We carried on after through Tincques, and eventually arrived at the little village of Monchy Breton. There we got settled into a 'posh' billet about an hour before the Battalion arrived. The other two cooks who had gone the day before met us. They had fixed things up well, for the cooker had a place with a cover, and there was a little barn for us to sleep in. The old folks at the farm presented us with some straw, and with this we made ourselves as comfortable as possible. We turned in as soon as we could, for although Macpherson and I had ridden the cooker horses for about four kilometres and had also ridden on the limber pole for some distance, we were just about whacked. My feet were none too rosy when we started, and the twenty miles we had had to cover by no means improved their condition.

The next morning Robertson and I had to turn out at 4.30am to make breakfast. By jove it was a wrench, so soon after leave, and I could hardly keep my eyes open; my 'trotters' seemed as sore as when I had gone to bed, and it was some time before I could get my boots on.

We stayed at Monchy Breton for a fortnight and, all things considered, had a fairly good time.

One evening 'D' Company held a concert, and it developed into quite a boisterous night. The rum punch that we made for the boys may have had something to do with the liveliness that prevailed!

The Platoon's rations used to be dumped in the yard of our billet in four uncovered heaps. One afternoon we scented a very offensive smell, and through the gateway of the yard there appeared a huge goat with thick shaggy hair. He proceeded to tuck in to the rations dump, but this of course was too much of a good thing, so 'Digger' Reavey very valiantly went forward with a broom to clear him away. The goat became annoyed, and very soon Reavey rushed off with the goat after him. After this we all joined in the fray, and had some sport trying to keep the animal away from our food. We threw things at him, and poked him with a broom, but the old brute had us beaten every time, and positively refused to budge. At times he would turn quite affectionate, but he would not let us presume upon his apparent good nature, and so long as we did not attempt to turn him out he was all right. While we were doing a little coaxing, and had in fact almost got him out of the yard, Hanson, an HQ cook, or as he was usually known 'Oscar', appeared on the scene. Oscar, although a very likeable fellow to put it mildly, had a very high opinion of his capabilities, and he evidently thought there was a good opportunity of displaying his prowess. He told us with great bravado that he would soon shift that goat 'at the toot'. The job was 'moleskin', a favourite word of his by the way. He went up to the animal, and gave it one almighty crack on the head with a bristly broom. The goat was staggered at first, and then cut up rough, and with one mighty rush tore after Oscar and soon had the heroic gentleman chasing round the yard. I never saw Oscar shift so quickly. At last he managed to clamber on to a big farm cart that was standing in the yard and was, for the time being, safe. After making several ineffectual attempts to get at him the goat next turned his attention to the rest of us, and very soon we were all posted on inaccessible perches. The animal stayed for just as long as it wished, and then just before dark ambled gently out of the yard, and we were able to come down from our perches.

On 9 February the Battalion left Monchy Breton by train. We left at 9am and got to Maroeuil about 4pm. When I arrived at the billet I was so stiff and sore that I could hardly move.

Early next morning the cooker was sent to the transport line with one cook, and the rest of us went up with the Company at 7am to a light railway. Although this was only about three hundred yards from the billets we had left we stood in an open field for four and a half hours before we entrained. So much for Army organisation!

We travelled in small trucks to 'Chanticler', as the railhead to the trenches was called. From there for an hour and a half, we plodded along a communication trench called 'Ouze Alley', till we came to the reserve line, known as the 'Red Line'. Our cookhouse was in 'Ouze Alley' siding. The place was so small that we could not pass each other in it. We stayed there for two days, and then moved to another position in the 'Red Line'.

The Germans shelled us during the night, and the shells came uncomfortably close. We stayed there for two days, and then the Company relieved the Fusiliers in the front line. We set out after dark, packed to the eyebrows with equipment etc., and toddled along the communication trench to the front line. After having marched for what seemed hours, our guide lost his way. It was the old, old story! After a long wait we got going again, but becoming rather fed up with the constant stopping, we cooks climbed out of the trench and walked along the top in the open. As soon as we arrived at 'Earls Street'—the front line—we had to get into the trench again, and there the mud was terrific. The parapets had collapsed in places owing to the recent rain, and in parts the mud came over our knees. By this time we were all exhausted, and what made matters worse was the fact that no-one seemed to have the slightest idea of our whereabouts. We climbed out of the trench again, and were then discovered by one of the Battalion guides. He took us to our new position, and one by one we dropped into the trench. In doing so I got caught up in some wire and, while struggling to free myself, the Germans opened on us with a machine gun. There was a violent push from behind; the wire and I parted company, and I arrived in a heap at the bottom of the trench with about four fellows on top of me. I picked myself up, and went along to the cookhouse in 'Brum Street'. There I rested for a while, and reflected on the British Army, and its brilliant system of guides!

From the 'Red Line' to the front line trench was only about two hundred yards, yet the trenches were so thick with mud, and the guidance so faulty, that the journey had taken us over four hours.

Work next day was decidedly uncomfortable, for the mud was everywhere; furthermore there were five meals a day to prepare. Later, however, there was a sharp frost which dried up a good deal of the wet.

On 17 February our dixies were carried down to a railhead called 'Boyne Dump'. The carrying party went down by the communication trench, but another cook and I decided to go over the top in the open as that was a quicker route. At 'Boyne Dump' the dixies were put on to trucks on the light railway. Piper Gordon and I had to push one of these trucks and, by Jove, it was stiff work. After half an hour's solid pushing we reached the 'Red Line', and there waited for a light engine. During this time we sat on one of the trucks. The Germans suddenly put shrapnel over, and as one large piece hit the truck on which we were sitting we decided to quit. Shortly after, an electric engine arrived and as soon as the trucks had been coupled on to it we set off in the darkness. It was a very exhilarating ride, for two or three times we were very nearly shot clean off the truck, and had to hang on for dear life. At one point a shell landed and only missed hitting the rails by about a yard. This happened in front of us, but luckily we passed the spot before the second shell arrived. We came to another sudden halt as the train very nearly ran into a limber that was lying across the line. Towards the end of the journey we travelled along a railway cutting. To say we travelled is to put it mildly, for the driver evidently 'had the wind up' and we fairly tore along. Articles fell off the trucks and it was indeed with a great sense of relief that we alighted at the 'Chanticler' terminus. There, a limber was waiting for us and, after loading our tackle, we set off behind it to the transport line at St. Catherine's (Arras). The next day the Battalion came down to 'West Camp', Roclincourt, and so we moved there with the cooker.

After four day's rest the Battalion moved up the line again, and Robertson and I went up with 'D' Company. We started off behind the limber carrying our dixies, and the Lewis gun. There was another exhibition of Army 'Red Tape' for when we arrived at one spot the Company was allowed to pass, but the APM (Assistant Provost Marshall) would not let us pass with the limber, as we had no duty pass. We had never even heard of a duty pass, so we had to go all the way back to Roclincourt, and go to the railway embankment at Bailleul by another route. I had a septic ankle at the time and could hardly put my foot to the ground. I stuck it for as long as I could, but eventually had to sit on the limber. When we arrived at Bailleul we unloaded just under a railway bridge. The arch itself was in a very groggy condition, and on it there were four railway trucks smashed to pieces by shellfire. We waited a long time for a carrying party to arrive for the dixies. My foot was causing me such agony that I decided to go off in advance, so gathering up my pack and equipment I staggered along the trench boards till I came to the cookhouse, where I found Reavey, and in a twinkling I had my boots off.

The CSM arrived with the programme of meals—and it was some programme, for there were eight meals per day and the times ranged from 4.45am till 12.30 (midnight). The Germans shelled us heavily during the night. We remained in that position for five days. A Company concert was held in a large dugout, and we made the usual rum punch.

On 27 February we moved up to the front line. There were two cookhouses there, one in 'Marquis' Street, a reserve trench, and the other in an advance post known as 'Oppy Post'. By this time the shortage of troops was being felt, and it was therefore found impossible to man the front line trenches properly. So, our old front line was abandoned, and the 'Red Line' was made the main line of defence. In front of this, at some considerable distance, parties of men were placed in posts at varying intervals along the divisional front, and these acted as sentry groups for the main line of defence behind. A big German attack was expected at any moment, and the men in the post received orders that when the Germans came over that they were to hold them as long as possible, and if they themselves became overwhelmed to make their way back the best way they could. The only way back would have been across the open, as barbed wire was placed on the top of the communication trenches, and the troops behind had orders to throw the wire into the trench at the first sign of trouble. Furthermore, our artillery were to put up a heavy barrage behind the posts, so that our fellows when retiring would have to pass through two barrages—our own and the Germans—in addition to the rifle fire of the oncoming troops. In all these circumstances therefore, it would have been a lucky man who got through!

'Oppy Post' was one of those delightful sentry post positions, and Robertson and I went there to cook for the garrison, about ninety fellows in all. The party set off along an endless communication trench, and we cooks brought up the rear with the party carrying our dixies. Of course after a time the inevitable happened and the Officer in charge lost his way. We of the rear party got cut off. So we got on to the parapet and, after sundry directions, set off over land to find 'Oppy Post'. We were carrying big dixies, and that did not help us as we groped along in the darkness. We fell into shell holes, and got hopelessly entangled with barbed wire, and to make matters worse it began to rain. This made the ground very slippery so that falling into shell holes was made quite easy. As we approached the front line the Germans put up Verey lights, and our progress was stopped by bursts of fire from their machine guns. We carried on until we reached the advance post, and found the whole Company in a large dugout. There were four entrances facing the German line, and at the bottom of one of them was our cookhouse. The general position was hardly enviable, for with the greatest of ease the Germans could have surrounded us at night and taken the whole bunch of us as prisoners. Furthermore, the German line was only about forty yards away, and within talking distance. At night too, their patrols had a habit of prowling round the back of our post.

As soon as rations arrived we turned in for the night, and then had time to reflect on the so called 'cushiness' of a cook's job. During the night there was a terrific 'shermozzle' and the post on our left, only two hundred yards away, was raided by the enemy.

The next day there was a shortage of water, for this could only be brought up to the post under cover of darkness. Fuel was also scarce, so Robertson went round the dugout knocking down any wood that was capable of being moved. The enemy left us alone for two days, but on the third night put down a heavy barrage behind our post. This meant that our way back was cut off, for the shelling was too severe to have passed through. We all had to 'stand to' with rifles and fixed bayonets. The Germans also 'strafed' the front of the dugout with 'Pineapples' (trench mortar shells) and later started putting gas shells over. Two fellows were wounded, and one was brought down into the dugout. He was hit rather badly, and lay in a pool of blood. There was a circle of shells bursting round us, and at any moment we expected the enemy to leap upon us. However, to our intense relief, the firing died down, and we received the order to 'stand down'. Three hours later the enemy started on us again, and put down a barrage behind us, and started shelling the post on our right very heavily. There was another 'stand to'.

The next day 'Jerry' gave us a pretty hot time of it. He 'strafed' our post with 'Minis' (giant trench mortar shells), and 4.2 shells. Their range was good, for they registered several direct hits. Everyone, except two sentries, were ordered to take cover in the dugout. Three out of four of the entrances to the dugout were blown in. I was sitting at the bottom of one of the shafts on an upturned dixie, when a shell landed at the top and blew in the entrance to the shaft. There was a rush of air, and I was lifted bodily off the dixies, and was sent spinning for about eight feet. Shovels were always kept at the entrances for emergencies, and as soon as there was a lull in the shelling the Company had to set about digging us out.

The enemy kept up a regular fire all day, but towards evening eased up. After dark the Kensingtons came up and relieved us, and I, for one, was mighty glad.

Robertson and I went down in advance with a carrying party, and at 'Boyne Dump' the dixies were put on to trucks. We went on to Roclincourt where we found the cooker. We took off our clothes for the first time in ten days, and slipped between blankets for a sleep. After a rest of six days the Battalion relieved the Kensingtons in the line and, as it was my turn to stay down, I went with the cooker to St. Catherine's (Arras). There I found the other Company cooks in a corrugated iron shed. The next night the Germans shelled us heavily with HE (High Explosives) and gas shells. There were a good many casualties round Divisional Headquarters for there were direct hits on some of the huts. The shelling was maintained for the best part of the night. At 4.30am we had to stand to' with the cooker ready packed, as the great German offensive was expected at any moment. Dawn broke, but 'Fritz' remained quiet. At about midnight we were all aroused by Tom Gallon, of the stores, who informed us that all matches had to be given in. At first we thought that this was a new form of humour, but found that it was true, and so gave up our matches—at least some of them! We discovered later that smallpox was rampant in the East End of London, and since Bryant and May's factory was at Stratford, the Army authorities were taking precautions to prevent smallpox breaking out among the troops.

On 16 March a number of the Battalion in the line were gassed by gas shells, and two of 'B' Company's cooks were affected, one of them being blinded. Two days after, the Battalion 'clicked' another bad packet, having between eighty to a hundred casualties. All the cooks from 'A' Company were gassed and sent to hospital.

At dawn on 21 March there was a thick mist, and the Germans launched their great offensive. There was a terrific bombardment, in which both sides did their share. The attack was not launched on our direct front, but on the Divisions on our immediate right flank. These comprised the 5th Army, under General Gough. They were driven back on a frontage of about five miles, and this, of course, left us in a mighty awful position, as at any moment the enemy could have made a turn and cut us completely off. However, as later events showed, they were going to deal with us a few days later.

Just as we were getting down to sleep that night, the Germans started to shell Arras and St. Catherine's. They were now doing a great deal of shelling on the back areas, even reaching as far as St. Pol, twenty miles behind the line. All this pointed to a lively time for us, and we knew enough about war by then to realise that interesting fact. Two nights later we were lying calmly in our billet in the middle of a field when there was a swish, and a 'Doughboy' landed on the side of the road. There was absolutely no shelter, so we simply had to lie there and hope for the best. There was an incessant rumble of guns all through the night until dawn. At about midday the guns burst out in another intensive bombardment. German planes endeavoured to get over our communications, but were driven back by our anti-aircraft guns.

On the afternoon of 26 March we were standing round the cooker, when an aeroplane came down to about fifty yards above our heads. We gazed at it with the usual idle curiosity when it heeled over and we saw the ominous Iron Cross on its wing, proclaiming it to be a German plane. We immediately gave the warning to one of our Lewis gunners who, incidentally, was asleep. Luckily another gun opened up, and the aeroplane sheered off and came to ground about a mile away.

In view of the very probable 'breakthrough' by the Germans when they attacked, Lewis gunners were attached to the various transport sections to act as a guard against German cavalry. Rumours began to circulate, both harrowing and discouraging, of the condition of the Divisions on our right flank that had been driven back. According to most of them our Army was well nigh shattered, and in full retreat. Strange though it may seem, we were not at all disheartened by these eports for we had really reached the stage when we did not care what happened. We should have made a fight for it, however, and should have disputed every inch of the ground. It was as well under the circumstances that such a spirit prevailed, otherwise we could not have borne the strain of the awful uncertainty. That the Germans were going to attack us we knew for certain, but the actual time and with what result was another matter.

On the 28 March the Germans launched their attack against our Division. At 3am they started off with a tremendous bombardment. Soon after the barrage lifted, and their hordes of three Divisions, carrying spare boots on their packs, came over against our men. Our own Division was weak in numbers, and was not considered strong enough to hold out. Consequently we at the transport line had orders at about 9.30am to pack up and, shortly after, the whole Divisional transport retired. On our rear limber a machine gun was placed to beat off enemy cavalry, and every now and then we looked back and kept our eyes on the ridge on which the fighting was taking place, for we expected any moment to see fast moving figures appear on the skyline. When we saw them we would know that the German cavalry would be on us in a twinkling, and what chance we should stand then did not bear thinking about. We travelled through Anzin, and at length came to a halt in a field just between Louez and Maroeuil, where we waited. The enemy cavalry did not appear, so we knew that the boys were holding out. News came through later that despite many fierce attacks the line was still intact, and that the Germans had been driven off.

They must have been very optimistic and certain of breaking through, for it was very unusual for them to carry spare pairs of boots into action. They were, however, beaten off by the 'Thin Red Line' and when the action was over the German dead lay round 'Oppy Post'—the Battalion's immediate front—in heaps; the number was estimated at two thousand. They were mown to pieces by our artillery and rifle fire.

The next day was Good Friday. The first news I heard was that poor 'Tich' Davidson, a 'D' Company cook, had been blown to pieces by a shell and nothing remained of him.

The Battalion was relieved that night and so Murrel, with 'C' Company's cooker, and myself, with 'D' Company's, set off to 'Ecurie Corner', Roclincourt, to make tea for the Battalion as it passed on its

147

way down. The first Company arrived about midnight, and from there onwards till nearly 4am parties passed. When the last of the tea had been issued we put the dixies on the cooker and set off back on our own. Dawn was just breaking as we rolled, a motley crew, into Mont St. Eloi. The other two cookers, 'A' and 'B', had gone on in advance and had served tea to the Battalion on its arrival. We turned in at last for a rest in a large French hut.

22 The Arras Caves—Blangy—Feuchy

On Easter Sunday we were reinforced by a draft of one hundred and eighty men composed of Durham Light Infantry, King's Own Yorkshire Light Infantry, and 'The Queen's'. 'The Queen's' were drafted to 'D' Company. This was the first occasion on which we had had drafts from non-kilted Regiments.

The next day the Battalion went out digging an entrenched position on the Arras–St. Pol road. This was in case of a breakthrough by the Germans. Three cookers took dinner over to them, and I was attached temporarily to 'B' Company. We stayed to serve tea and then returned.

On 6 April the Battalion moved again, and we followed to an aerodrome just between Maroeuil and Duisans. This had been evacuated because of shelling. However, as we were merely 'cannon fodder' we were billeted in the hangars. The whole of 'D' Company and the transport, about two hundred and fifty men in all, were put into one of the hangars.

There was another move next day, and just before we started the rain came down in torrents. We halted on a ridge outside Wagonliu, and waited for darkness, when we carried on two deep through Arras till we arrived at Ronville, a suburb of Arras. A long delay then followed, during which 'Jerry' strafed us with shrapnel and gas shells. After some time we got moving again, and arrived at the entrance to some caves. There was a cry of 'gas', and we had to put on our gas respirators. When the gas had passed off we entered the mouth of the caves. We descended to a considerable depth by a shaft cut in the chalk, and at the bottom walked a long way in the bowels of the earth. We were billeted in a huge cavern which opened out of the tunnel along which we had walked. The whole Brigade and also Brigade HQ were billeted in the various caverns around. There was accommodation for at least four thousand men. Water was laid on, and the crowning feature of the whole place was the electric light, which dimly illuminated the caverns. The caves were so lofty in places that they resembled cathedrals; the extent seemed to be unlimited and they stretched for miles. It was said that they went as far as Wancourt, and that was ten miles away. Furthermore, the Germans were supposed to be in the other end. There was one serious disadvantage, apart from the unhealthy atmosphere, for the caves had been dug out in such a way that there were no corners; consequently it was impossible to get out of the draught. Large chunks occasionally used to fall from the roof without the slightest warning.

There was also a light railway running along the main tunnel. We made enquiries as to the whereabouts of the cookhouse, and learned that it was on top! This was very cheering news, especially as the place was particularly hot from the shelling point of view. I asked one of the Canadians who, by the way, we were relieving, if he could direct me to the cookhouse. He took me to the top of the shaft, but would not go any farther. His parting injunction was 'don't hang about'. Very encouraging, to say the least. After floundering about among a row of shattered houses, I discovered the cookhouse in a broken-down cellar. We were not allowed to sleep there though, as the place was not provided with gas screens. 'Digger' Reavey and I waited for the carrying party to bring our dixies along. When we had got everything shipshape for the morning we returned to the caves for a sleep. We had just turned in when the gas alarm was sounded, and I had to make a dash for my gas mask.

The next day we had to shift to another part of the caves. This meant the same amount of packing up as if we were going ten miles. I went in an advance party with the 'Skipper' to take over our new positions. This time I 'scrounged' a cookhouse in the caves at the bottom of one of the airshafts. There was an inspection by the Colonel next morning and when he saw our fire he very nearly exploded, and fairly went off the 'deep end' at us, for he said fires were not allowed in the caves. It was pointed out to him that there was a shaft, so after having put the fire out, we were told we could relight it! 'B' Company's cookhouse, which was on top, was shelled, and 'Bill' Kinch was gassed, as was also a cook of HQ Company. 'C' Company's cooks were also shelled out of their cookhouse. Later on 'B' Company cooks came and worked with us. After a few days the caves began to make us feel limp, and we simply longed to get into the open air. To make matters worse there was glorious sunshine on top.

On 13 April the Battalion relieved part of the 167th Brigade in the line. No cooking was possible in the sector to which they went, so that we were told to go to the transport line. We walked through the caves till we came to a spot where they were connected with the main sewer under Arras. We walked for a long time through this sewer until we came out on top at the Levis barracks in the centre of Arras. From there we carried on to Dainville where we were lucky in getting a lift on a motor lorry to Warlus, and from there we walked to Berneville where we found the cookers.

After a couple of days, arrangements were made for cooking in the trenches, so Reavey and I once more turned our faces towards the line. I was feeling very unwell, and had nearly lost my voice. We arrived at the support trenches and were then informed by the CSM that there was no cookhouse, and he did not know why we had been sent for. It was close on 2am so we went along to the stretcher bearers' shanty, a shaft of a dugout—and there, in a huddled heap, snatched a few hours sleep. The next morning I went round the trench with the CSM looking for a likely place for a cookhouse. I found an old disused dugout shaft, and decided to turn it into one. It was choked full of rubbish, and had first to be cleared out. When everything was prepared we had to hand it over to 'C' Company, for that evening we moved up to the front line trenches. There a portion of a dugout was set aside for us, but we were only allowed to cook at night, since it was the first occasion on which cooking had ever been done in that part of the line, and the Battalion did not want to advertise the fact to the enemy lying just in front of us. The dugout was a German one, and so the entrance faced their trenches; consequently great care had to be taken not show any light when cooking at night. On 19 April 'C' Company went 'over the top' at 4am to capture a German post. The Pioneers fixed a gas curtain over the shaft of the dugout in case of 'accidents'. The raid was successful, and the booty consisted of eight machine guns. After this our Company was ordered by the Division to retire as reprisals were expected, no doubt. At 4pm Reavey and I went off in advance back to the caves at Arras carrying a big dixie between us. At one point we were spotted through a gap in the parapet, with the result that the Germans very nearly blew us to smithereens with a well placed shot. At the end of the trench we struck out on to the open track. Needless to say we did not linger by the wayside, for the track was under observation. After about two hours we reached Ronville, and there descended into the caves. The Battalion was relieved by the Queen's Westminsters and joined us later in the caves.

The next morning our dixies were loaded on the Lewis gun limber, and we walked down behind it through Arras. Just before leaving the town we ran into some mustard gas, where 'Fritz' had recently been shelling. We got to Berneville and there found the cookers in a large shed. The Battalion arrived at 8pm and we issued tea to them. When I got up next morning I found that my voice had completely gone. This was evidently due to the whiff of gas the previous day, which had put the finishing touch to it. Two days later the Battalion returned to the caves. 'Digger' and I, meanwhile, remained at the transport line. On 12 May we moved up with the cookers to Dainville, and the Battalion arrived there from the line early the next morning.

We remained at Dainville for six days, during which time there were four inspections.

On the evening of 18 May we moved off again. The cooks were specially ordered to turn out in full uniform, for what reason I could not fathom, as it was pitch dark when we moved off. However, it was not for the cooks to reason why! We arrived at Arras and stayed for a few days with a gentleman named Monsieur Lesage, at No 56 Rue de Baudimont. As a matter of fact, he was not at home at the time, but in a way this was better since we could do as we liked with his property. M Lesage's absence was, no doubt, due to the very delapidated and unhealthy state of his house for it was badly knocked about by shellfire. Next morning we had a good look round our new apartment. We came to the conclusion that it was a 'posh' billet, and that we could have settled in there for the duration of the war. What particularly filled our hearts with glee was the finding of two tables, one large and one small, and one delapidated chair, the seat of which had long since departed. It had, however, been repaired with pieces of wood, and so for our purposes was as good as one of Maple's best. The finest find, however, was a large mirror in which we could see ourselves at full length—not, by the way, that the sight of ourselves as others saw us helped to inspire confidence! There was an old flower vase, not complete of course, for nothing seemed complete out there. We filled the vase with flowers picked from the neighbouring garden and placed it with great pride in the centre of the table.

Mr Lesage must have been a gentleman of portly appearance, for we came across a lounge suit of his. We tried it on by turns and in every case there was ample room for development. Robertson was the most favoured among us in the way of girth, but when he put that suit on he looked hopelessly underfed.

Later on we came across a large iron bath. This we dragged out into the yard, and Sergeant Cowl (of 'D' Company) when he saw it said he would have a bath. He stripped, and while he stood there displayed in all his natural glory, we 'sniped' him with any missile that came to hand. Robertson, meanwhile, steathily crept upstairs, and from a room in the upper storey let fly the contents of a large water can on the unsuspecting bather beneath. The rush of water coming from a height, very nearly brained Sgt Cowl, and he fell down flat.

We came across a top hat—it seemed to us almost prehistoric. Robertson donned it and an opera cloak and went outside, while we hailed imaginary taxis for him. This I might add caused quite a sensation among the Company fellows who were billeted on the other side of the street.

After three days we moved up again, and this time 'Digger' and I went with the Company. We arrived in a trench beyond Arras known as 'Blangy Support Trench', and there found the cookhouse to be a corrugated iron shed.

On the fourth night 'Jerry' started to shell the ration track to the right of the cookhouse. He kept this up for some time, sending over salvo after salvo. He then switched round, and very soon shells were bursting round the cookhouse. Since our roof would not have stopped a bullet, let alone a shell, we had to chase out mighty quickly. After a time the shelling ceased, so we returned to the cookhouse and turned in for a sleep. 'Fritz' started his game again during the night, but luckily we came to no harm. Early next morning the Germans put down a very heavy barrage over our front and support line. For over an hour there was an incessant rain of shells round our cookhouse, and there were ominous thuds in the trench as the jagged pieces of shell struck the earth. We stuck it for a time but eventually had to clear out as things got far too hot. Later we returned, and then went to sleep with our tin hats and gas helmets handy. It was lucky we did so, for about 2am I was awakened by a crash. Gas shells, shrapnel and HE shells were coming over in a continuous stream. We were warned by the Officer on trench patrol that there was gas about so we took refuge in a dugout shaft. It certainly looked as though the Germans were going to attack us at daybreak, and so our own artillery got going as well, and the 'shemozzle' then developed into one terrific roar. However, daylight dawned without any further trouble, and peace reigned once more—for a time, at least.

At 10pm the next day the Battalion moved up to relieve the 4th Fusiliers in the front and support lines.

Our dixies were taken up by a carrying party, and all the way up the Germans 'strafed' us with shrapnel and gas shells. We walked along 'Cemetery Trench' till we got to a deep sunken road down which we went to some quarries by the river Scarpe. There we found quite a roomy cookhouse. It had been used by the artillery, and was perched high up on a bank next to the railway line. Leading down from the floor of the cookhouse was the shaft of a small dugout. The artillery cooks evidently took no risks! Shortly after dark next evening we had cause to bless this dugout, for we were shelled heavily and had to disappear helter skelter below ground. After a time there was a bombing raid on each side of us, so that 'Fritz' had to stop shelling us and confined his attention to the raiders. We were then free to watch the raid. It was a glorious sight—from a distance. Shells bursting, Verey lights and Golden Rain lighting up the whole area.

The Company used to be drilled in a little valley just below us. We thought that this was a mad procedure, and fairly asking for trouble and, sure enough, one morning a German plane hovered over, and evidently spotted them, for very soon 'Pipsqueaks' were dropping all round the Company, and they had to make for cover. Number 16 Platoon was having foot inspection at the time and had to dart off without any boots or socks on. They must have had a prickly journey, for there was plenty of loose barbed wire strewn about. After that little excitement drilling in the valley was abandoned.

The Germans gave us another pasting, and two fellows were wounded just outside the cookhouse, and were brought in to have their wounds attended to.

The German observation balloons looked right into the valley, and so of course, could see everything that we did. At 3am on 3 June there was a heavy bombardment, and for over an hour the shells were dropping round the cookhouse and dugout. One landed right on the dugout, and the whole place shook, but luckily there was just sufficient earth on top to hold it up. The earth steps leading to the cookhouse were completely blown away, and the shelter around us received nasty 'packets'. The enemy had evidently sent petrol shells and we had to wear our gas masks.

At 9pm we moved up to relieve 'B' Company. Our cookhouse was in a sunken road just south of Feuchy, and the Company was in trenches just a little way in front. Communication during the day was impossible as the ground was under observation, so our cooking was done at night. We slept in a Nissen Bow hut with an earth covering. We each had a stretcher to sleep on, so that things were quite 'posh'. We were there for six days during which time I was very nearly put out of action. One evening 'Digger' and I had just made tea for the boys; to make carrying easier, this had as usual been poured into petrol cans. These were left in the cookhouse till the carrying party came for them. Unfortunately, they were placed too near the fire, and one of them began to boil. To prevent it from bursting, and so probably wreck the cookhouse, I went to unscrew the metal stopper. There was a tremendous rush of scalding tea which caught me on the right side of my face. I ducked, and the boiling stream rushed down my back and right shoulder. I then dropped to the floor; by this time the boiling tea was hitting the roof of the cookhouse, so that by dropping I got out of range. The pain was awful so I ripped off my shirt and immediately rushed outside in the cool, as the heat from the fire made the pain unbearable. 'Digger', with great presence of mind, rubbed the whole of the twenty-four hour butter ration over my burns. It happened to be salt butter and I gave a frantic leap. One of the stretcher bearers dabbed me with a field dressing and ointment, and the fellows then carried me to the hut, laid me on a stretcher, and left me to rest. The next day my face was swollen and my back was raw, and it was only by a fraction of an inch that my right eye was missed. After a time the scalds got better, but it was a painful process, as the weight of my pack and equipment caused me agony. The fact that I was not scarred for life, I always think, I owe to 'Digger' Reavey.

On 8 June the 7th Middlesex Regiment relieved us and we went down to Dainville, where I found the other two cooks billeted in a Nissen Bow hut. We were out of the line for nine days. Brigade sports were held at Berneville, and 'Digger' and I went over with the cooker to make tea for the Company on the Sports ground. Baths were built in Dainville, and on the occasion on which I went to them the Germans shelled and caught some of the bathers, wounding quite a number.

The next time the Battalion went up the line 'Digger' and I stayed with the transport. The epidemic of Spanish influenza, which had been making great ravages among the troops in the surrounding villages, reached us. Brunton, a 'C' Company cook, and 'Digger' fell victims and were sent to hospital. The rest of us were suffering from sore limbs and headaches. Soon others were down with the 'flu. I developed a temperature and lay in a ramshackle barn on the second row of a tier of wire beds, shivering all day and night. On the top tier and over me, chickens ran about, and my presence underneath did not in any way prevent them from performing their acts of nature whensoever the occasion arose. Some kindly disposed cook brought me some dinner—stew! He meant well, of course, but I felt like throwing it at him. After two days, as they were short handed on the cooker, I staggered to my feet and pottered around as well as I could. I felt as weak as a rat, and later had to go back to my wire bed. The next day I felt a bit better and by degrees my strength gradually returned to me.

On 6 July the Battalion came back to Dainville, so the cooker was moved there, and we made tea for the Company on its arrival at 4.30am. While we were at Dainville 'Digger' returned to us from hospital.

23 Château de la Haie-Tilloy—Boiry—Boyelles

The Battalion moved up to Arras on 8 July to take over from the Kensingtons, and Robertson and I went in advance to our old billet at 56 Rue de Baudimont—the residence of the absent M Lesage. After two days there, we marched again behind the Company back to Dainville, and the following day carried on further to Fosieux, where we slept the night on the ground in the open, between a mud oven and a boot scraper! At 9am the following day we took to the road again, and arrived at Chelers, where we remained for three days, just long enough to be deceived into thinking we were out for a rest, but on 18 July we moved off again to a place called Château de la Haie. Here we were put into huts (Camp St. Lawrence) in the park adjoining the Château.

The cookers were drawn up in the open under some trees, and in front of a shed in which our stores were kept. There must have been a tremendous number of troops in the surrounding district, for I attended performances given by three different Divisional Concert parties, 'The Volatiles' (these, by the way, had a full orchestra and gave performances in a large hut called the 'Irving Theatre'), 'The Verey Lights' (20th Division), and 'The Snipers' (24th Division).

About midnight on 25 July I was awakened by a terrific crash just near the billet. The hut shook, and I was in a dazed condition wondering what on earth had happened when I heard the ominous purr of an aeroplane engine. Shortly after, it was followed by the noise of a bomb falling through the air. There was a terrific and ear splitting crash, and the roof of the hut was riddled like a pepper box with shrapnel. The stars could be seen through the rents made by the pieces. Goodby, a stretcher bearer who was sleeping about a yard from me, was wounded in the head. We could not show a light, as the Germans were still hovering overhead. All night long their planes came over, and all we could do was to lie low and take our chance. Some time after the crash the Companies were ordered to leave the huts, and to go into the woods to sleep. Robertson and I went along with them. Soon after, however, the rain began to fall, so we stealthily stole back to the hut and spent the rest of the night there. We were the only two in the hut, as the Company stayed in the wood all night.

In the morning we were able to see the effects of the raid, and the sorry mess there was. Our cookhouse had been levelled to the ground, and hardly a brick was left standing for the bomb had dropped right in the middle of it. The Sergeants' Mess cook who had been sleeping in a little shanty attached to the cookhouse had been killed. 'A' and 'B' Company's cooks had a shelter about ten yards from the spot. Johnson of 'A' Company, had the muscles of his arm torn from the elbow to the wrist. There were also casualties in the second hut from our own. All our kit was strewn amongst the debris and little by little we gathered this together. I was lucky in recovering most of mine undamaged, for others had their tunics torn to shreds. My original diary was picked up out of a pile of bricks and a piece of the bomb had gone right through it. I usually carried this in my tunic breast pocket—that night was a lucky exception. The cookers were standing about seventeen feet away from the shed, but pieces of bomb had hit ours in a number of places. One of the wheels, and also the supporting pole, was cut in two. Dixies were punctured, and metal bowls and knives were twisted up like paper. The whole of the Battalion rations were destroyed, and the Quartermaster had to telephone to the ASC dump for more. We had cut up about one hundred and fifty rashers of bacon for the Company's breakfast, but these were nowhere to be seen. Great planks had been shot into the trees into inaccessible spots, and remained suspended there. Like the 'Sword of Damocles' we expected them to fall on us at any moment. The previous night I had lent Robertson my watch, as it was his turn to make breakfast. He had hung it on a nail in the cookhouse, but when he went for it after the raid all he could find hanging on the nail was its ring—the watch itself had gone; verily does time fly!

After we had been at Château de la Haie for about a fortnight we moved up. 'Digger' and I entrained with the Company on a light railway just outside the park gates. Seated on small open trucks we had a sort of scenic railway view as we passed Villers au Bois, Mont St. Eloi and Bray, till we detrained at Anzin. The cooker then served dinner, after which it returned to Berneville. The Battalion then carried on to Arras, and for a few hours were housed in Levis Barracks. 'Digger' then went up with the Company to the line to relieve the

Canadian Scottish while I waited at the Fish Market with a cook from each company to go up later. A ration limber eventually arrived, and after having loaded our dixies we set off to join the Battalion. I had great difficulty in finding 'D' Company, and was gaily travelling along the Arras-Cambrai road behind the limber when I met Sergeant Baxter of our Company who told me I had gone beyond the British front line, and was in 'No Man's Land' and heading for the German front line!

The limber was immediately turned round in, I may say, record time, and after having found the Company we unloaded. 'Digger' was in our new cookhouse in the middle of 'Devil's Wood' (Tilloy). It was by no means a healthy spot, for it was a half-submerged cellar and would not have stopped anything. The Germans shelled us all night, at half hourly intervals. Two nights after, a shell very nearly finished the cooks, for it fell not three yards from us.

On 3 August the Kensingtons came up after dark and relieved us, after which 'Digger' and I attached ourselves to Number 16 Platoon and went down with them to Arras. We found 'D' Company billeted in Rue d'Amiens. The cookhouse was a carriage shelter with a flight of steps to a cellar, over the entrance to which was a gas curtain. Our sleeping place was a stable, and at 2am we turned in with our heads under the manger. There was a large school near our billet, and in its library we found a number of English books, so we set ourselves up with new literature. In the basement of a convent close by we came across a cooking range about fifteen feet long. The whole concern was a mystery to us for we could not fathom how it worked, as it stood in the middle of the room and there was no chimney or outlet at all. We converted it to our own ideas, however, and were rewarded with success, for out of its unfathomable mystery we produced a dinner for one hundred and forty men. If the ghost of the chef of that range had seen the liberties we took with it, he would have received a severe shock to his ghostly system.

On 8 August the Battalion took over the sector of the line to the left of Tilloy Wood, and so Robertson and I went up with the Company. Our cookhouse was at the bottom of a dugout shaft thirty feet deep. It was so dark that we had to burn candles night and day. We remained there for five days, and then moved up further to 'Blangy Support Trench'. We occupied that position for six days and they were very exciting ones. The next morning at 5am the 'fun' commenced.

159

Robertson and I had a little shelter in the trench—all there was to protect us was a sheet of corrugated iron. The rest of the Company were down a dugout. A salvo of 5.9 shells came over us; we lay in our shelter and at first they did not worry us much, but suddenly there was a crash and a shell landed so close as to threaten complete annihilation of our shelter, and so we had to scamper off like a couple of rabbits. When the shelling had ceased we returned to our shelter. We had no sooner done this, than the shelling began again. After a bit things quietened down, and we had a walk round the trench inspecting the damage. We came to a shell hole in which there was an unusual kind of yellow powder, and a peculiar smell. I took a good sniff and declared that there had been gas in the shells. This was something new, for gas had not been sent over in HE shells before. Robertson took a sniff and said it was not gas, and a long argument ensued during which we both took a few new sniffs and then went along to the dugout to call the Gas Corporal. When he appeared we set the case before him and he came along to the shell hole. He took a mild sniff and then chased off like made yelling 'Gas'. The sequel to this came later in Army orders, for that night every unit was warned that the Germans had started to put gas over in high explosive shells.

I was very lucky to get away with that 'packet' as lightly as I did, for I must have taken quite a lot of gas into my lungs with the many sniffs that I took. The ground had become so impregnated with the gas that all the troops were ordered out of the area, and the trench was put out of bounds. I was unwell during the morning, and had a shocking headache, and completely lost my voice, and soon Robertson was affected in the eyes. At 10.30pm the Germans made a raid on our front line, and when our guns answered the SOS signal it was like all hell let loose. The enemy put up a gas barrage over our trench, and we had to lie with our gas masks on. The shelling kept up for about an hour and a half.

The next day Robertson was worse, and had to be led to the Aid Post with a bandage round his eyes, for he could not bear the light on them. There was a continuous stream of water running from my eyes and they were extremely inflamed and very sore. I was in chronic pain as my head, throat, eyes and lungs ached unmercifully. In addition the mustard gas had burnt me severely in a certain delicate part of my anatomy that is not usually displayed in public! We had forty casualties from the gas, one of which was fatal. Most of them got to

England or the base. Robertson did not return to us until some months later. I, like a mug, thought I would hang on to the Company, and so did not go to the Aid Post. I paid for it, though, in pain and suffering for about a fortnight. Not having reported myself in the first instance I was, of course, prevented from going to the MO for treatment afterwards because the Army had such peculiar ideas that, instead of appreciating one's efforts to carry on, the unfortunate individual would have received a very severe 'telling off' for not having reported sick in the first instance. Our Army may have been a wonderful machine, but like all machines it lacked commonsense and sympathy.

I had to get well, therefore, without attention. I did at last get better, but it was a mighty agonising process.

All the food was condemned, as it had been contaminated by gas, and the cookhouse was shifted to another positon. I managed to get to the new position, but I literally had to drag myself along over the ground to get there.

On 17 August the Division was relieved and the 10th Battalion Scottish Rifles took over from us. We moved down to Berneville, and I was thoroughly glad to turn my back on that particular sector.

Early next morning the whole Battalion travelled on the light railway from Berneville to Nougelette junction, and then marched for four hours in the blazing sun to Mazières. Those four hours were agony to me. The perspiration caused by marching in the hot sun aggravated my burns terribly and, what with that, lungs full of gas and sore feet, I felt fit to drop when I at last staggered into the billet.

Two days afterwards we moved again, to La Couchie. The next morning my throat was very bad. I coughed a great deal, and before every cough had to press my hands hard on my lungs to relieve the pain. It was a blazing hot day, and I could only move by great effort. The Battalion was on a five minute notice to move, and at 7pm the alarm was sounded to leave for the line. This meant another move, and oh! how I cursed those moves. The cookers went on their own to Berles au Bois, and there pulled in to an open field. We cooked meat and bacon, and this was sent up on the ration limbers. We discovered some caves in the middle of the village and, on entering, found them crowded with soldiers and civilians. Most of the civilians had taken their bedding down there. German planes came over during the night.

At 4.45am on 23 August, the Battalion went into action, and so after dinner we moved up to Bretincourt. We drew up just outside the village close to a wood, and spent the night in an old artillery forge. The place was riddled with shrapnel and bombs. Nine horses had been killed there, and their skins were hung out on a line.

On 24 August we moved up after dark to the Battalion. For about three hours we carried on past a stream of ammunition columns, ambulances and tanks. At one part of the journey German planes hovered over the road, firing machine guns on the ceaseless line of traffic below. Luckily, we just missed the murderous hail of bullets, for the plane cleared off just as we came up to it. The road was also bombed, but there again we were lucky. Away behind us we saw the fitful spurts and lurid glare of flames mount up every few minutes as bombs dropped on the same column of traffic of which we formed a part. Those who had passed the spot shortly after told us that it was the scene of carnage, for over fifteen motor lorries had been blown to bits, and pieces of men and horses showed all that was left of an ammunition column.

At the end of that eventful journey, the cookers were drawn up on a railway embankment just behind the trench from which the Battalion had started on its recent attack. We made tea, and then lay down by the side of the cooker wheel for a sleep. The Germans kept up a continuous shelling all night, and once they came so close that we had to make for cover in an old dugout about fifty feet away. We had just got comfortably settled there when the 169th Brigade Staff arrived, and bundled us out, and so we had to go back and sleep by the cooker wheel. We spend another night there, during which it rained in torrents, and in addition 'Fritz' dosed us with gas shells, so that we had to get our masks on. There was a heavy bombardment early next morning in preparation for the taking of Monchy le Preux.

We shifted again on 27 August and passed through the recently captured village of Boiry till we found the Battalion in a trench just beyond. All around there were signs of a hasty retirement by the enemy, for German trench mortar guns were left absolutely intact with shells ready at the side, and there were dead Germans lying about the village.

The Battalion moved further up at night, but we remained at Boiry in an open field and went to sleep in a little hole dug in the side of the trench. Next day our horses came up, and took the cooker back to the

162

transport lines just behind Boileux au Mont. We stayed there for a day, and then all the Brigade cookers moved up to their respective Battalions. We got to within about half a mile of Croiselles and waited there for two hours. It was then found impossible to get the cookers up to the Battalion as the congestion of traffic caused by the ammunition columns was too great. We drew on to a track, therefore, out of the way of the passing traffic. At this point, however, the connecting pole of our limber snapped, the cooker nearly turned upside down, and there was a deluge of boiling water. One of the transport fellows was sent back for a new pole. In the meantime, we crawled into an iron shelter close by and waited. Dawn broke before the new pole arrived, and as it was then too late to make tea for the Company we were sent back again. The next day the other two cooks went up to the Company with the ration limber to cook in the trenches, while I stayed with the transport.

The Battalion was relieved on 31 August by a Regiment of the 52nd Division, and so we moved up with the cookers to a trench just in front of Boyelles (where we stayed with the Battalion for five days). The Company arrived thoroughly exhausted at 6.30am the morning after our arrival, 'D' Company returned about sixteen strong with no Officers, and only one Sergeant (Sergeant Ball MM).

24 Cambrai

At 4.30am on 6 September the whole Brigade took the track through Croiselles to Vis-en-Artois, a village about half a mile from Monchy le Preux. There we were billeted in an open field just outside the village. A day or two previously the Canadian transport had drawn into the same field, and had been immediately shelled by the Germans, and nine out of their ten cookers had been blown to smithereens. Their remains could be seen strewn around the field, and the air was foul with the stench of dead horses. This was so absolutely overpowering that although we could stand practically anything, yet in sheer self-defence the Company had to set to, and cover over with earth the mangled remains of the horses nearest to them. Even after this, though, the steady breeze carried the odour of those horses further afield. We had to stay there and eat our food with that foul stench always in our nostrils. There was a terrific thunderstorm soon after, and we got thoroughly soaked. This would not have been so bad if the rain beating on the ground had not stirred up those dead bodies, and so made the smell if anything worse. German planes were over all day and, in view of what had happened to the Canadian cookers, we had orders to camouflage ours.

The village was shelled all day on and off, and another of our observation balloons was set alight; in fact this seemed a daily occurrence now. After dark the Battalion moved further up and I went with the Company, while the cookers remained at the transport line. After a long march over wet ground, saturated with gas, we took up a position about fifteen hundred yards in front of the village of Eterpigny. There, in the shaft of a German dugout, we improvised a cookhouse. We made tea just before dawn, but the smoke was absolutely murderous for there was no current of air to carry it away.

The next day there was a gas alarm, for 'Fritz' was shelling the area at the back of us, and there was a liberal sprinkling of gas shells.

On 11 September the company moved down just as darkness was closing in. Another cook and I waited behind for a limber to carry our tackle. We set off down the road at midnight, over a shocking track thick with mud, falling into shell holes and trenches in the pitch darkness. We arrived at last at Remy where we found the Company in little bivouacs along a sunken road. The next day was perfectly miserable, for the cooking had to be done in the pouring rain and, in addition, 'Fritz' shelled on and off all the time with shrapnel. On 13 September the Battalion moved down into Brigade reserve at Tilloy. The Company went down by buses, but 'Digger' and I trekked behind the cooker with the transport. When we got back to Tilloy we found that the Battalion had taken over the same position in which Robertson and I had been gassed a short time previously. This time, however, things were different, for instead of having to crawl about as if we were only there by kind permission of the Germans, we now had the cooker itself drawn up on top of the trench, and there was no fear of being sniped or gassed. Verily we appeared to be winning at last!

On the fifth day the Company travelled by buses to St. Rohart, near Monchy le Preux, while 'Digger' and I followed by road with the cooker. On the way we met a string of thirty wounded horses on one long rope. They were in the hands of the Blue Cross. It was quite a pitiful sight to see these poor old warriors with their bandages. One nag had holes about the size of half crowns all over his flanks.

On arrival we served dinner and tea to the Company, and afterwards went back again to the transport line at Guémappe. The Battalion moved up to relieve the Canadians in the line. All the horses around us at Guémappe were tied near shell holes, so that in the event of a bombing raid they could be placed as far as possible in a shell hole for cover.

The transport of the London Rifle Brigade, who were to the left of us, had two men and forty of their horses killed in one raid. After that, orders were issued that all horses were to be put in the shell holes at night. Getting the nags in used to cause some fun and excitement, for they seemed to be under the impression that they were in for some mysterious form of torture. It was a weird sight at dusk, for all around one could see countless horses' heads, with apparently no bodies, poking up out of the ground.

One plane unloaded twelve bombs on the road to our left. Our searchlights 'fixed' him, and a good shot from an anti-aircraft gun brought the invader down—not before he had done damage though, for the pilot had hit a troop train in Arras station, and there had been one hundred and forty casualties. Three blasts on a whistle used to be the signal that 'Jerry' was approaching, and then out had to go all the lights. The Arras-Cambrai road used to be his special target, and our field lay adjoining this.

On 1 October we moved along the never ending Arras-Cambrai road. The Germans saw to it, however, that our tramp was not monotonous, for just as we were passing Vis-en-Artois they started shelling us with 'heavies'. Having successfully passed through that little encounter we ran into another 'packet' farther up the road. They put five or six shells within three yards of the road, and we took cover behind the limber as far as possible. One of the shells hit an ammunition limber in front, and as we passed we saw the driver by the roadside dead, with half his face blown away. The four leading mules had escaped injury, and had been cut loose. One of the mules, however, harnessed to the limber itself, had been hit and was dying in a sea of blood. Poor brute, it was piteous to see it. Its partner lay quietly at its side, while its mate breathed its last.

We reached Cagnicourt and took up a position in a large wood outside the village. During the afternoon several batches of prisoners passed us, escorted by Lancers.

We dug a hole near the transport line, and made a roof over it with a limber sheet. It was as well that we did so for soon after dark the German planes came over. They dropped a bomb on the wood behind us and it was a case of 'to your tents, oh Israel'!—and we made for the hole in the ground. The searchlights picked up the plane, and with our heads sticking out of a hole we saw it slowly approaching us. It came directly overhead, when I heard a rush through the air, and knew that a bomb was on its way. It fell and exploded with a crash on our horse lines. A dump of cordite had been set alight, so that in the red glare of it I could see all that happened. All our horses were tied in a long line on a rope fastened to two big posts in the ground. The horses stampeded and broke loose. Two of them with one of the huge posts to which they had been tied dangling between them, set off in a mad career straight towards the hole in which we were. In a moment they would have fallen on top of us, with goodness knows what result. Luckily I just had time to rush out and dart in front of them, waving my arms and shouting. This headed them off and they shot off into the blackness of the night. As soon as the plane had gone, the horse pickets went immediately to the horse line.

For half an hour we heard revolver shots as the poor wounded beasts ere put out of their misery.

In the morning I went to see the spot where the bomb had fallen. We were indeed lucky for the hole in which we slept was only a stone's throw from the horse lines. The sight was horrible, for the ground all ound was thick with blood, and horses in contorted attitudes, and ith most gruesome wounds lay dead. Three had been killed utright, and nine others beyond hope, had been shot. Luckily not a nan was hit, though there had been some miraculous escapes. One orse had the lower part of its leg blown off, another lay with a nostril hot away, and an eye taken clean out. Several had been hit in the tomach, and their intestines had been dragged out. Besides the welve put right out of action, three others had been hit, but as there vas a chance of recovery they were not shot. One, the Colonel's harger, had a piece of shrapnel just near the kidney. The other two ad been hit in the neck and one of them was permanently blinded in ne eye. It was a sight to see those animals patiently standing there nd making such a good fight of it.

Later on in the day prisoners captured in the Cambrai fighting assed us on their way down. On 5 October we moved up with the ooker, and took the road through Marquion, over a pontoon bridge vhich had just been made by the Engineers over the Canal du Nord. This was a fine piece of work, and consisted of three bridges side by ide; two over pontoons and capable of bearing infantry in fours and ight transport, and the third a stouter structure for heavy artillery. The process by which the heavy bridge had been made was ingenious, ut simple. Three of our tanks had been driven into the Canal, one ver the other, and over this temporary foundation a sturdy bridge ad been built. It was indeed a feat, for the Canal du Nord was one of he enemy's strongholds, and the whole work had been carried out nder fire. Owing to the efforts of the Engineers, we were able to pass he canal with the whole of our transport.

We carried on, and halted at Sauchy Lestrée and there drew the ooker into a sunken road close to the Battalion Headquarters. When he Company arrived we made tea and porridge for them. We spent he night in a German dugout; this was a 'posh' affair, and was fitted throughout with wooden beds. Unfortunately, however, the dugout was too far from the cooker, so next day we had to build a shelter for urselves in the sunken road.

The next day there were wild rumours that the Germans were

making overtures for peace. The cheering effect of these was somewhat counter-acted by the terrific bombardment that broke out at night which continued till dawn. We came in for the return fire from 'Fritz' and the shells burst all round our shelter. The Battalion moved up after dark, and the cookers were sent back to the transport line. Another cook and myself went up the line with a limber carrying our dixies. We arrived at our destination, an embankment just outside Oisey-le-Verger. There had evidently been some excitement, for 'Fritz' had gassed the area badly, and the cookhouse reeked of it. A poor fellow was lying outside on a stretcher dead.

We unloaded, and got things shipshape. As soon as we had done so we had orders to take all the foodstuff to Company Headquarters as that was outside the gassed area. Two of the stretcher bearers gave us a hand in carrying the stuff. As a bank of loose earth about forty feet high had to be scaled the fun was fast and furious. We arrived at last, and found the dugout crammed full. There was only just room enough for us to sit on the stairs, one on each step, and we sat like that until the next morning, at which time we returned to the cookhouse to prepare breakfast.

We could see Cambrai in the distance burning all night.

The next day the Company shifted to a cellar in the village, and we went along there and fixed up a cookhouse. We scrounged a couple of German wire beds and fixed up a table and last, but not least, found a large cane travelling trunk, and in this we decided to keep our rations. We lit a beautiful fire in a brazier with some German coal nuts that we discovered, and everything was quite cosy. We were no sooner comfortably settled, however, for the night when the Company received orders to move again. We were left behind, so I went along to Battalion HQ for orders. Later on a limber arrived and took our tackle to Battalion HQ.

Just after dawn the next day, we were sent back to the transport line at Cagnicourt. We could see Douai burning in the distance. On 11 October we moved up with the cooker to Rumancourt, and there fixed ourselves up in a chalk quarry.

We stayed at Rumancourt for four days and then the cooker, together with two cooks, moved down to the transport, while another cook and I left with the Company. I had a poisoned ankle, and well I knew it by the end of the day. The Company marched while I hobbled to Marquion. There we lined up in a swamp by a railway track, and waited for a train. The swamp, with the water over our boots, would not have been so bad if the train had turned up on time. It had been derailed, however, and we had to wait while things were put right. The swamp by this time was getting monotonous. All the time the pain in my foot was almost beyond endurance, and I could hardly lift it up. After a wait of ten hours the train arrived, and at midnight we got on board. I dozed off and on waking found it was 8.30am and we were just starting. It took four hours to do fifteen miles and if that was the train's normal speed, I cannot for the life of me imagine however it had ever managed to get derailed.

At last, stiff and sore, but nevertheless cheerful, we steamed into Arras. We marched to the Baudimont Barracks, where the other cooks who had gone on in advance with the transport, were waiting to serve up breakfast.

25 The Final German Retreat

Our stay in Arras this time was quite pleasant, for by now the town was practically out of the War zone. Large parties of French refugees from the villages that had been recaptured from the Germans began to arrive daily, and were housed in the Schram Barracks.

My poisoned ankle was still bad, and I spent a few days hobbling about in a slipper.

A Battalion concert was held, and Hallowe'en was celebrated as usual.

We should have been in Arras for a Divisional rest of about a month, but after a fortnight this was suddenly curtailed, for news came through that the Germans were retiring all along the line. On 31 October 1918, therefore, we set out to follow the enemy on the final drive that was to send them back into their own country. Naturally by this time, their resistance was feeble, and it really became a matter of following them up—cautiously, of course, as there was always the possibility of an ambush. Throughout the whole advance our Division followed, in conjunction with a Canadian Division. The two divisions, so to speak, played leap-frog. We would get in touch with the enemy, and either drive them back or take over the village evacuated by them and then the Canadians would pass through us and carry on with the good work. The cookers followed the Battalion a little distance behind, and when it stopped for the night we would go up and serve meals to the men. When they advanced again we followed at the allotted distance. When the call came, the transport set out by road, and 'Digger' followed with the cooker. The rest of the cooks went with the Battalion in motor buses. The whole Division travelled in one long column of buses, and this set off at about 9am along the Arras-Cambrai road. As we passed the villages recently evacuated by the enemy, we could see the wilful devastation and destruction wrought by the Germans. Cambrai was a heart rending sight, for bridges had been blown up, and huge masses of masonry and twisted ironwork lay about. The huge lock gates had been destroyed, and the New Zealand Engineers were repairing them as we passed. Everywhere buildings had been wantonly burned. The REs were busy locating mines which the Germans were known to have set before leaving. One billet marked 'OK Safe 177 REs' showed where at least one mine had been discovered and rendered harmless. Houses had been pillaged and there were heaps of furniture everywhere. Part of the town was still burning as we passed through.

When we reached Douchy we alighted from the buses, and our first step was to find a cookhouse. We came across a suitable place for the cooker in a yard. The folks in the cottage close by fairly overwhelmed us, and could not do enough for us. We asked for wood and they produced stacks of it.

Our sleeping place was an attic in a house about a hundred yards away and when we retired for the night the people in the house gave us a thorough welcome. The village had been in German hands for the last four years, and the relief of the folk was quite touching. They were refugees from Cambrai, and their house had been utterly destroyed, and ransacked. They invited us into their living room and made us coffee. All offers of money they stoutly refused, for they said 'if the Germans had asked, and had been refused, we should have been sent to prison, and so you are welcome'—and one could see that they meant every word they said. One woman of the village, they told us, had been imprisoned for declining to supply coffee, when a German refused to pay for it.

We spent a thoroughly enjoyable evening and, if it had not been for the pathetic element, I could have laughed outright at times. What tickled my 'funnybone' was this. There were five of us present, and our combined knowledge of French was not guaranteed to make our remarks very intelligible. After having drawn very heavily on my brain power, I just managed to trot out an intelligible French phrase. That did it! The French folks fairly jumped on me, and mistook me for a linguist, and I had a lively time of it for the rest of the evening. Of course my chums very discreetly withdrew from the conversation, and left me to it-they would! I did all the spluttering, and it was some spluttering at times, especially as our conversation drifted to the German U Boat campaign. Those dear folk honestly thought that the British had not a ship left. But I told the tale and, after I had done so, I rather think that they were under the impression that we had millions of ships, and they learned for certain that Britain still ruled the waves.

There were two elderly ladies and two old gentlemen. One of the gentlemen did not seem capable of talking, hearing, or even comprehending, so of course he dropped out of the conversation at a very early stage. I had rather a near squeak with him, though, for hearing that he smoked a pipe, I offered him my tobacco pouch for him to take a pipe full. Unfortunately he seemed under the impression that I was giving him the lot, pouch and all. I rather prized that pouch so by a strategic move I withdrew the pouch and offered him a cigarette instead. I began to have great doubts as to whether the old boy was as slow as he looked. The other old chap had a face full of whiskers—I never saw such fungus—and when he spoke all one could see was something moving. It may have been that by the time his words came through his whiskers they became somewhat frayed, for I could not understand a word he said. French is bad enough when straightforward, but when it has to pass through a whisker screen it is more difficult still to understand. Of course, as luck would have it, he would talk the most; I used discretion and always agreed with him, and when I thought the answer should be 'yes' trotted out a non-committal 'oui' or vice versa. I must say I was wonderfully lucky in my replies. One of the old dames got so excited when she spoke that she looked like the villainess in a Lyceum thriller, so I adopted the same attitude towards her—toujours la politesse! The other old dame took things more calmly, and I could get on all right with her. She had an absolute horror of the Germans, and it was from her that I gleaned most of my information. She herself had been in prison for three days for having a candle alight at 9pm and was also fined ninety francs for having gone to another village, only about two miles away. Before we finally retired for the night they all insisted on us having cocoa.

Another incident which stands out in my mind was the day when we had rabbits in rations and were instructed to make rabbit pies. This, of course, was impossible on a cooker so we had to look for a suitable oven, which we eventually found in a farmhouse. We used the faggots that we saw lying there to light the fire in the oven while the old farmer was screaming 'blue murder'. After the fire had been lit we had to wait until there was sufficient heat before we put on the door. I asked how did one know when it was hot enough and was told that you put your arm in the oven and if it came out with all the hairs burnt off then the oven was hot enough. This I accordingly did and the hairs burnt off all right and I was lucky to still have an arm left!

172

During all this time the old fellow was still creating until I told him in no uncertain tone to 'shut up'.

We duly put the rabbit pies in the oven, shut the door and hoped for the best. When we thought the pies should be about ready we opened the door and took them out. I had a look at them and then said I thought they should look shiny and so we poured 'Ideal Milk' over them and then pushed them back into the oven and, oh boy, did they come out shiny! After we had finished with the oven we had to rake out the ashes with a long rake and it was then that I realised the cause of the old fellow's excitement, for there in the middle of the ashes was a tin box containing, I presume, the family jewels that the farmer was hiding away from the Germans.

'Johnny' Hall was our Battalion butcher and I said to him one day, 'that was a funny animal you had yesterday'. He said 'What do you mean.' I replied 'Well, it must have had five legs and "D" Company had two of them.' I think he got the message. Some time later, for some reason he was not able to do the butchering and so asked me if I would do it for him, and with an eye to the main chance I said I would. I hacked into the carcass with a cleaver, and when I had finished I am sure that no professional butcher would have recognised the joints. However, 'D' Company did well for meat that day!

We stayed at Douchy till 2 November when we moved on again. The whole of the Divisional transport travelled in one column, and the Battalion marched on ahead. The transport travelled across country, and the going was very rough as the mud was absolutely thick. Two or three times we were brought to a long halt because the limbers stuck fast in the mud. At last we arrived at the village of Maing. The other three Companies were billeted in a sugar refinery, but poor old B . . . 'D' Company 'clicked' an open field. When night fell it began to rain, so we cooks disappeared and spent the night in the refinery.

The next night the Germans retired, so we were off again. It was absolutely pitch dark and the road was terrible. We floundered along, and occasionally fell into shell holes. At every sudden halt it was impossible for the drivers of the limbers to see that the traffic in front had stopped, so that at every step we had to jump sideways very quickly, otherwise we should have stood a very sporting chance of being run over by heavy draught horses coming up behind and nearly touching us. As it was, the pole of the limber behind once or twice just grazed my head. All things considered, I was mighty glad when we rejoined the Battalion outside the village of Famars.

We served tea to the Company and then pulled back to Battalion HQ which was situated in an old farmhouse. There, we cooked meat and bacon and after that had been sent up to the Company we turned into the farmhouse for a 'kip'. At 8am the next morning we were off again. Passing Valenciennes on our left, we wended our way slowly along the main road. At one spot there was a particularly long halt, as it was found that the crossroads had been mined. The REs were just digging out the mine as we got up to them. When the detonators had been removed we passed on. Later on a 6in howitzer stuck fast in a shell crater on the road, and so held us up again. Ten horses struggled their utmost, and eventually the great gun was pulled out. We passed dead Germans and horses, and at one spot there was a German cooker badly mauled, with a dead horse in harness hooked to it. The crossroads at Saultain had also been mined, and the crater caused by the explosion made it very difficult for us to pass by. We pulled up in a village to water and feed the horses, and to fill our dixies. We carried on later and arrived at Estreux, where we found a regular welcome awaiting us from the inhabitants. The enemy had left only the previous day, and the relief of the civilians was great. They came out cheering, clapping their hands and crying. One old gentleman would persist in raising his hat to us, as though we were so many Field Marshals. That travel-stained and soot begrimed cooks should come in for such a mark of respect was, I need hardly say, unexpected, and completely took our breath away.

There was a pathetic incident, unfortunately, for a little French child, hearing the noise of our guns as we were approaching the village, thought that the Germans were returning, and the shock killed the poor mite; a crowd of weeping women stood outside his cottage door as we passed.

The cookers were pulled up in a yard, and we found a 'posh' little house with a French stove in the kitchen. This we soon got going, and we sat round in style. We found some straw, and placing this on the ground had a comfortable 'kip'.

Early next morning the late occupants of the house returned to take over possession again. They said there was no need for us to go, for which piece of information we were truly thankful. The folks, two women and a little girl, stayed and chatted with us, but soon the position became rather awkward, for it was evident that they had returned for good. We thought at first they were going away, and were coming back later. Luckily I had dressed before their arrival but the other cooks were still in their blankets on the floor, and undressed. They slipped their things on under the blankets, and emerged with smiling faces fully clad. 'Digger' was in a sore plight, for he was lying right at the feet of the two women, and his clothes were in the next room. Suggestions that he should wrap himself round in his blanket and boldly walk out of the room, he treated with scorn. At length we decided on a ruse. I picked up a tin of Maconachie Meat and vegetable ration, and putting this under my tunic went out of the room; a minute later I returned and stood in the doorway. I attracted the ladies' attention, and asked them if they would like something to eat. They came across to get the tin, and in a twinkling 'Digger' got up and shot out of the room. Soon after he reappeared with his anatomy decently covered, and a seraphic smile on his face.

On arriving at the billet the previous night I had seen an old Frenchman outside gesticulating wildly and pointing to the cross-roads. He tried hard to tell us something, but we could not be bothered to listen to him. The next morning when I went out I found the reason for the old boy's excitement, for the REs had just finished digging at the crossroads, and as I appeared one of them held up to me the fuse of a mine that had been laid there. The old boy had seen the Germans laying this mine just before they left, and he was trying to tell us. Bless his heart! We had lain there all night within a few yards of that mine!

We were just getting down to sleep that night when we received orders to go down to the transport line. It was pitch black night when we set off; we reached Saultain, where the cookers were drawn up outside a hangar at a German aerodrome. There was no accommodation for us, so we looked for a billet ourselves.

Working round the cooker next day was undiluted misery. The mud came over our boots; very soon they were filled and, in addition, the rain was pelting down. After dark in pitch blackness, we loaded rations on the cooker and took to the road again. After about an hour in the perishing cold, we came to a block in the road, caused by a motor lorry having stuck fast in the mud. In trying to pass, 'A' Company's cooker limber capsized. Everything had to be unloaded, and in the thick mud it was some job. It was our turn to pass the stranded lorry next and, horror of horrors, our cooker got jammed between the lorry and the bank. The limber was on one wheel leaning on the lorry. I expected any moment to see the wheel collapse. The driver decided to rush the limber, and trust to the limber righting itself. 'Digger' and I, therefore, put our shoulders to the side and some of the others hung on to the drag rope attached to the limber to keep it from going over completely. If the limber had gone over 'Digger' and I would have been badly crushed, and I did not relish the job at all. However, with a shout to the driver, and a caution to 'Digger' to give me room to jump clear if anything happened, we tried our luck. There was a lurch, and an agonising wriggle of the whole machine and, with a sigh of intense relief, we saw the cooker ride clear of the lorry right side up. After this we carried on, and arrived at Sebourg about midnight, to find another block in the traffic. Luckily we were able to pull out of the line, and into a yard.

The Company did not arrive until 7am next morning, and while waiting we walked about kicking our heels, trying to get warm. After we had served breakfast we got down for a sleep. Our billet was a large barn with twenty five horses in it. The only place I could find in which to sleep was a passage covered with about two feet of manure. However, 'beggars cannot be choosers' and so I lay my ground sheet on the manure and getting down to it went to sleep. It was jolly warm too, and before long I was lying in a cloud of steam. Later on, the artillery, who were in the yard, had sudden orders to move up, and came into the billet to take out their horses. I was asleep at the time, but I awoke with a start to find a great horse towering over me, and just about to put his hind leg down on me. Needless to say I moved like a rabbit. In the rush the artillery men had not noticed us in the gangway, and they brought out their horses four abreast. When they had left we went into the stable, and four of us slept behind a little partition with horses on the other side.

Early next morning there was a rumour that the Germans in front of us had evacuated their position in the night, and later we had to pack up hurriedly and follow them up.

We passed the Belgium frontier at Rousin. There were flags everywhere, and all the inhabitants were mightily pleased. In one village the Germans, before evacuating, had driven all the Belgian horses into a field, and shot them all, and as we passed the inhabitants were cutting steaks off the dead animals.

The roads had been blown up, so that at times we were considerably delayed. We stopped at Angreau about midday, and came to a long halt, as a bridge across the river in front had been blown up, and we had to wait while the Engineers repaired it. As we had a wait of about eight hours before us, we went to a barn in the village, for the cold was so severe. After dark we loaded up the rations for the Company on a limber. I was carrying a big box of bacon, and in the darkness fell right up my waist into a shell hole full of water. My boots filled and my clothing was soaked. However, I could not undress, and so my clothes eventually dried on me. When the bridge was ready we set off again. Getting over was a ticklish business, for on one side there was no balustrade at all, so that a false step would have meant that the cooks and cooker would have plunged headlong into the icy cold river. It was pitch dark, so I went in front of the horses with a small flash lamp, and very gingerly the driver followed me. Having got across safely, we carried on to Autreppe, and arrived there in the early hours of the morning. We had a hayloft to sleep in, and as there was a supply of straw we slept quite well.

The next day the weather changed for the better; this was very welcome, for the intense cold had been extremely trying. The Germans were still falling back, but they did not stop anywhere long enough to allow the infantry to get a really good smack at them. The main body would retire, leaving machine gunners to act as a rearguard. As soon as our advance troops came in touch with them the gunners would leap on horses and scamper away.

On the 9 November the enemy had retired again and we had to follow them. We stopped at Erquennes, the transport line, for an hour, and then carried on to the Battalion. By this time the enemy had retired beyond the devastated area, and the surrounding country was quite fine. On all sides cattle were grazing in the fields. We found out later that this was due to the fact that the Germans had driven off the cattle from the parts they had previously occupied. We had got too close upon their heels, and as they could not take them with them any longer, they had turned them loose in the fields.

We arrived at Rinchon, and were billeted there in a large farm. The farmer had had nineteen horses, but the Germans had taken eighteen of them, and left only one. They had also killed one hundred and fifty of his poultry.

We were in luck again, for we found a barn full of straw.

177

At 9.30am on 10 November we moved off with the Company in the direction of Mons. The roads were severely damaged in this area, making travel very tedious and hard. The civilians grew very excited, and ran along at our side shouting 'Vive Angleterre'. At one place, Coron, the girls gave us bunches of flowers as we passed.

At 2pm we arrived at Blaignies, and the cooker was drawn into a farmyard. There were some cows in a shed, and I have never seen such sorry looking objects for they were nothing but skin and bone. We were forbidden to drink any of their milk, as the Germans had injected all of them before leaving the village, and thus poisoned the milk. We 'clicked' another billet with straw, and this was particulaly acceptable as the cold was bitter. By this time, too, we were feeling the effects of hunger, for food had been getting terribly short, and we were living on starvation rations. The ration lorries had not been able to keep up with us owing to the bad state of the roads and the railways had been completely destroyed, for the Germans had put explosives under every rail joint. We were two days in advance of our rations. It was announced in Battalion orders that night that for the future rations were to be brought up by aeroplane, and dropped near us. Further, that in order to be able to move more quickly and harass the enemy, the big guns were to be left behind, and the light guns were to have double teams of horses. The infantry were to dump their packs, and were to carry double ammunition. We did not look forward to the future with any feeling of exhilaration. Everything seemed to be double, except rations—and food, or the lack of it, was our greatest concern just them!

The German retirement had been so well carried out that we could not rid our minds of the feeling that they had 'something up their sleeves' for us when we got to their country. It was one thing to give up an enemy country, but quite another to have one's own towns destroyed. We had been able to cross the Canal du Nord only with great difficulty, and then only under fire. So what was there in store for us when we endeavoured to cross the Rhine? With these gloomy forebodings, therefore, we turned in to sleep.

I got up next morning, 11 November 1918, to make breakfast for the Company. Soon after, an artillery man on a horse came careering through the village, shouting that the war was over. Frankly, I thought the strain had been too much for him, and that something had snapped in his brain. Outbursts of half-hearted cheering ollowed, and eventually official orders were sent round to the Companies that at 11am the 'cease fire' was to be given as an armistice ad been signed.

Folks at home apparently went frantic with joy and excitement. It eemed to be taken for granted that the war had finished, although an rmistice in the strict sense of the word is only a truce. That we fellows did not conduct ourselves like a crowd of maniacs, as many at home eemed to have done, was no doubt due to the fact that we looked upon the armistice merely as a truce—a temporary cessation of ostilities. We had faced the Germans for many weary months, and new by experience that they were fighters, by no means to be despised. Furthermore, we had followed them mile after mile in their etirement. It was never a retreat, for that suggests disorder. Considering the conditions and what it was up against, the German Army's retirement was truly wonderful, and it was not until the very ast that the enemy began to show signs of disorder, and that they vere being hunted.

There were many folks at home who thought that the war should have gone on a little longer—another few days might have brought about a debacle—but I thank God that we did not have to go on like so many military greyhounds. Of one thing I am certain, the enemy would at times have turned at bay and have shown his teeth—and the bite, even of a dying dog, is not pleasant. 'Truce' to us spelled time for the Germans to reorganise, and that would leave a tougher proposition to be faced. Frankly I had had enough, and felt thoroughly war weary and in that respect I was not alone.

About 10.55am on Armistice Day, our artillery began to open fire on the Germans, and for five minutes every battery on the whole of our front was sending over salvo after salvo. The air was rent with the whining and shrieking of shells as they hurtled over our heads. All this, of course, sounded very much like permanent peace! However, when 11am arrived the noise began to die down and a comparative calm prevailed. I discovered later that the final five minutes burst of firing was not due to any war-like spirit on the part of the artillery, but to the fact that every shell not used had to be carried about; empty shell cases were of course, dumped. When the 'Cease Fire' order was sounded the artillery, stout hearted fellows, did not want to be bothered with live shells that would have to be carried, so they adopted the perfectly legitimate method of disposing of them in action. My utmost sympathy went out to the Germans, poor devils; it was rough luck on them when the war was practically over, for many must have passed over to the Great Beyond in that final burst of fire.

For days afterwards we could hear distant rumbling and explosions. These were the numerous mines laid by the Germans being exploded by our engineers.

We stayed at Blaignies for a fortnight, and all during that period the cold was intense. We had a change of billet and it was a change for the better, for our new one contained a little French stove. An aged couple lived in a cottage close by. 'Hubby' was terribly henpecked and all day long the old lady used to nag, nag, and nag him. The old boy usually took it quite steadily, but one afternoon in sheer desperation he went out to see a funeral!

There was a good deal of sickness in the Battalion, and this was attributed to the bad water in the village, so we were moved to Eugies. There is no doubt that there was something wrong with that water, for whenever we boiled it a thick green scum used to form on top. We skimmed this off from time to time with a ladle and when we put the tea in, fortunately the green turned to brown. Otherwise, I rather fancy that the Company fellows would not have enjoyed their tea. It was a case of 'where ignorance is bliss'.

At Eugies we were billeted in the Mairie, in a small room that was as cold as ice. Opposite us was the room in which the civil marriages used to take place.

While we were at Eugies, a Belgian 'kiddie' found a mills bomb and childlike, drew the pin and threw the bomb. This burst and wounded an old Belgian.

On 27 November we moved to Givry, a little village close to Mons. We were billeted in a house, Number 14 Rue sous la Cimetière, and slept on the floor in the kitchen. We were very comfortable there, and the folks did all they could for us. I had many a chat with them and they told me, among other things, that they had not tasted meat for four years, and for months had eaten nothing else but carrots, morning, noon and night. America had sent food supplies to the Belgians, but the Germans had commandeered everything. The civilians were left without food, and only had what they were able to conceal from the harvest. The villagers during the last two months, had been dying daily of starvation. The Germans had taken boots, brass fittings from the doors, windows, etc. jewellery and even clothing, leaving the civilians in some cases without even a shirt.

The expression on their faces was sufficient testimony to the veracity of their statements. With a final sigh, they would remark 'ah, your people in England can never understand'.

The village fire brigade turned out one day for practice. They were not in uniform, as the Germans had commandeered their brass helmets. They had an old manual engine, and the speed was nothing out of the ordinary, but it caused us an occasion for a good laugh. When the practice was over, we lined the route and gave three hearty cheers. These 'pompiers' were not at all pleased, for I am afraid we ruffled their dignity terribly.

We moved again to another billet, Number 20 Rue de Toudroir. While there I was ill and the old lady doctored me up. She fairly soaked me with coffee until I dreaded to see her go near the stove on which the coffee pot always stood. She produced an egg and insisted upon my eating it. Offers of payment she stoutly refused, although eggs in the village cost a shilling each.

On 14 December I left the Battalion on my final leave. I travelled thirty miles by motor lorry to Valenciennes over bad roads. The journey would have been accomplished in half the time if it had not been for the driver who would keep stopping to give the Belgian girls a lift. From Valenciennes to Boulogne was a hundred miles, but the train took thirty six hours to cover the distance. At Boulogne I boarded the SS *Victoria* and after a rough passage landed at Folkestone. A couple of hours later I was once more back in London.

At one period during the war I was granted an extra sixpence per day efficiency pay, for what I never found out. In addition I received another penny a day for every year or part of a year that I served on the Western Front so that I was one of the highest paid infantrymen in the British Army at the princely sum of one shilling and tenpence per day.

A fortnight before I arrived home on leave, my brother had died, and I went up to the Territorial Army Headquarters in the City, to get an extension of leave on compassionate grounds. There was a long queue there, but the first person I spotted was wearing a Hodden grey kilt and turned out to be a fellow called Lindsay who had been in my Company. He asked me what I wanted and he said 'What about demobilisation'. Of course I was all for it, so he took away my leave warrant and brought it back so covered with Official stamps that it was difficult to read the original warrant. I asked him what to do next and was told to wait for orders. On 1 January 1919, I had instructions to go to Wimbledon Common Camp, where I handed in my rifle and equipment and received my discharge papers.

Shortly after, I walked out once more a civilian, and profoundly thankful that physically I was A1 and that despite many months of nerve-wracking experiences I was still 'clothed in my right mind'.

*　　*　　*

After having marched round France and Belgium for nigh on four years, I made a vow now that I was back in civilisation that I would not walk a mile more than necessary. I am happy to say that I have religiously kept that vow to this very day!

Index

Abbeville 15, 17, 52
Agny 113
Amiens 82, 93
Angle Wood 86, 87, 88
Angreau 177
Anzin 158
Archicourt 114, 117, 123, 124
Army, 5th 125, 146
Armentières 93, 110
Arras 112, 113, 115, 116, 119–125, 142,
    145, 146, 149, 151–3, 157–9, 165,
    166, 169, 170
Arras Caves 149, 151, 152
Arques 126
Autreppe 177

Bailleul 134, 142, 143
Bapaume 126, 128
Battalion, No. 4 Entrenching 15
Bayencourt 69–72, 77–80
Berles au Bois 161
Berlincourt 132
Berneville 123, 151, 152, 155, 158, 161
Beumetz Le Cambrai 131–3
Beuraines 115–9, 123
Bethune 23, 52
Beugny 127–133
Blaignies 178, 180
Boileau Woods 89
Boileux au Mont 163
Boiry 162
Bombs 28, 33, 37, 41
Boulogne 99, 100, 121, 124, 125, 138,
    139, 181
Boyelles 163
Bray 83, 139, 158
Bretincourt 162
Brigades
    1st Guards 17
    3rd Brigade 39
    167th Brigade 101, 106, 123, 126,
        130, 135, 150
    168th Brigade 63, 101
    169th Brigade 162
Buneville 124

Cambrai 159, 164, 166–8, 171
Cagnicourt 166, 168
Canadians 150, 164, 165, 170
Canal du Nord 167, 178
Chalk Pits 32, 36
Chateau de la Haie 157–8
Chelers 157
The Citadel 89–91
Coigneux 71, 73, 119
Combles 89
Commissions 49, 92
Cooks 64, 74, 78, 144
Courts Martial 50
Corbie 82, 90, 91
Croiselles 162, 164
Croix Barbée 107, 109

Dainville 123, 151, 152, 155–7
Daours 82
Death Valley 86
Divisions
    1st 17, 58, 59
    17th 81
    51st 132
    52nd 163
    56th 60
Douchy 171, 173
Doullons 15, 62, 81, 112
Drucat 81

Ecourves 133
Ecurie 134
Equihen 125
Erquennes 177
Estaires 95
Estreux 174
Etalemenite 95
Etaples 52, 54
Eterpigny 164
Eugies 180

Famars 174
Feuchy 155
Flixecourt 61
Folkestone 99, 100, 138, 139, 181

Foncquevillers 73
Forceville 60, 61
Fremicourt 126, 127, 129, 131
Fremont 93, 94
Fricourt 83, 91

Gas 29, 88, 106, 129, 134, 144, 145,
    149, 150, 152–4, 160, 164, 168
General Hospital, No. 26 52
Givry 180
Gommecourt Wood 71
Gouy en Artois 113, 119, 120
Guemappe 165

Hallincourt 94
Hallow'en 49, 96, 129, 170
Halloy 68, 81
Hebuterne 68–72, 78–81, 119
Hindenburg Line 117
Hocquincourt 94, 95
Hohenzollern Redoubt 41, 46
Hulloch 21, 33, 34, 41, 44, 46

Ivergny 113

La Basse 23
La Brebis 35
La Buissière 50
La Couchie 161
La Grande Pacart 106
La Gorgue 99–103, 109
La Rutoire Farm 34, 46
Lagnicourt 126, 128, 129, 131
Latrines 54, 113
Laventie 95, 96, 99, 100
Le Havre 13
Le Transloy 126, 133
Leuze 89
Lespesse 24, 25, 27
Lice 14, 16, 20, 106, 120, 136
Liencourt 124
Lillers 17, 24, 25, 46, 48, 50, 52, 58, 59
London Scottish
  'A' Company 43, 44, 72, 77, 80, 90,
    101, 107, 108, 114, 115, 131, 146,
    148, 158, 175
  'B' Company 38, 45, 71–3, 88–101,
    114, 127, 128, 145, 148–150, 154,
    156
  'C' Company 20, 39, 41, 45, 46, 63,
    72, 77, 79, 91, 92, 101, 115, 118,
    128, 129, 147, 150, 151, 156
  'D' Company 19, 27, 44, 63, 64, 69,
    70, 72, 73, 76, 78, 80, 85, 90, 94–7,

    101, 105, 106, 116, 124, 126, 127,
    131, 140, 142, 147, 149, 153, 159,
    163, 173
Lone Tree 30, 31, 39, 40
Longpre 17, 61, 95
Loos 27, 29, 35

Maing 173
Mametz Wood 83
Maricourt 85, 92
Maroeuil 138, 141, 147, 149
Mazieres 161
Mealte 91
Merville 95, 106, 112
Military Police 72, 138
Monchy Breton 130, 139, 140
Monchy Le Preux 162, 164, 165
Mons 178, 180
Montenescourt 123
Mont St. Eloi 133, 139, 148, 158
Moule 124, 126

Neuve Chapelle 107
Neuville Vitasse 117, 118
Noeux les Mines 37, 38, 46

Oisey le Verger 168
Oppy Post 143, 144, 147
Ouderdon 126

Pas 70
Petit Houvin 123
Pont du Hem 104, 105
Poor old B. . . . D (P.O.B.D) 8, 173
Poperinghe 126
Posts
  Dead Dend 95, 96
  Euston Dump 109
  Hougemont 95, 96
  La Bassee Dump 107
  Magpies Nest 129
  Moggs Hole 107
  Picantin 95, 99
  Sandbag Corner 112
  Winchester 104

Rats 110, 111
Regiments
  4th Army Corps 81
  Army Service Corps 25, 61, 101
  1st Black Watch 17, 21, 31, 50, 59
  1st Cameron Highlanders 17, 21, 50,
    59
  Canadian Scottish 159

184

INDEX

1st Coldstream 17
Duke of Wellington's 112
Durham Light Infantry 149
Gloucestershires 35, 50, 75
Highland Light Infantry 17, 86
Kensingtons 63, 80, 88, 134, 144, 157, 159
King's Yorkshire Light Infantry 149
3rd London Fusiliers 89, 126, 130, 135, 141
4th London Fusiliers 121, 154
London Rifle Brigade 165
1st London Scottish 11, 17, 32, 50, 55, 63, 76
18th Manchesters 119
7th Middlessex 121, 155
8th Middlessex 74, 101
New Zealand Engineers 170
The Queens 149
Queen Victoria Rifles 72
Queen's Westminsters 151
The Rangers 63, 69, 70, 96, 97, 99, 104, 105, 127, 128
Royal Engineers 22, 69, 71, 78, 97, 108, 167, 170, 174, 175, 177
Royal Fusiliers 63, 70, 76, 79
Royal Horse Artillery 34
Scots Fusiliers 21
1st Scots Guards 17
Scottish Rifles 161
Signal Corps 28
South Wales Borderers 34, 43
Remy 164
Reninghelst 126
Rinchon 177
Roclincourt 134, 139, 142, 145, 147
Rouen 13–15, 35, 48, 54, 58
Rousin 176
Rugby Football 25
Rumancourt 168

St. Amand 68, 70
St. Omer 124
St. Riquier 81, 82
Saffron Walden 12, 13
Sailly le Bourse 46, 72, 77, 79
Sailly le Sec 82
Sauchy Lestree 167
Sebourg 176
Simoncourt 120, 123, 133

Somme, The 71, 74, 81, 82, 83, 91
Souastre 68, 71, 74
Soultain 174, 175
Southampton 13

Tanks 85, 86, 115–17, 131, 167
Telegraph Hill 115
Tilloy 98, 121, 159, 165
Trenches
  Blangy Support 153, 159
  Brum Street 141
  Casement 89, 90
  Cemetery 154
  Chimpanzee 84, 86, 88, 89
  Cross Street 78
  Curly Crescent 19
  Earls Street 141
  Edgware Road 97
  Fence Alley 46
  Marquis Street 143
  New Welcome Street 77
  Ouze Alley 134, 141
  Park Lane 98
  Pip Street 20
  Red Line 141–3
  Rotton Row 98
  Whiskey Street 78

Trones Wood 89

Urinoir 65–8

Valenciennes 174, 181
Varennes 16
Vermelles 17, 20, 22, 23, 28, 34, 38
Vermin 14, 16, 20, 106, 110, 111, 120, 136
Verquin 22–4, 27, 29
Victoria Station 99, 100, 138
Vielle Chapelle 112
Villers sur Simon 61, 62, 66
Vimy Ridge 115

Johnny Walker 30, 34

Wancourt 123, 150
Watton 126

YMCA 14, 54, 55, 127
Ypres 126, 129